The Strangers Project

What's Your Story?

TRUE EXPERIENCES FROM COMPLETE STRANGERS

Brandon Doman

Foreword by Frank Warren, author of *PostSecret*

HARPER DESIGN

An Imprint of HarperCollins Publishers

Foreword

As I write this foreword, I'm sitting next to a stranger on a cross-country flight. My seat-mate and I have exchanged a few formalities but nothing more. In our continuing silence, I reread more of the extraordinary stories Brandon has been able to capture and curate in this book.

The more I read, the more I want to take action, like Brandon, and invite this woman next to me—whom I will likely never see again—to share her story with me. I want to ignore what my mother told me many times growing up, to "never talk to strangers," and learn more about who she is.

> *When I was a little girl I remember sitting in the backseat of my mothers car staring out into the LA traffic looking into the cars of the people passing by and wondering what their stories were, who were these strangers?*

Years ago, I started my own unlikely art project, inviting strangers to mail me their secret anonymously on a postcard. I believe my project, PostSecret, and the Stranger's Project are part of a larger tradition of people who value the everyday experiences of ordinary people—including Studs Terkel, who painstakingly collected oral histories from common folk through the second half of the last century, up to Brandon Stanton's daily street portraits of "Humans of New York."

As I walk about the city of my childhood I keep thinking/ hoping/dreading(?) that I might cross paths with my homeless father.

When I asked Brandon to tell me the goal of the Strangers Project, he said, "I wanted to create a physical space that would invite people to be curious and exploratory—a space that would create pathways and a structure in which people would open up organically. I didn't want to use prompts like, 'Tell me your favorite memory'—I thought it would be far more interesting to see what we share when given a blank canvas and an invitation to be present." By taking this organic approach, Brandon discovered raw authenticity and a wide diversity of experience, which also led to some surprises.

The day after home coming I took a bra from your room.

What I didn't expect from this book was to be so inspired. Before our flight touched down, I found the courage to talk to the stranger the world had randomly placed next to me. She opened up and described her most meaningful travel experience, which involved her son, a starlit sky, and families of sea turtles.

To quote Brandon, "I believe that everyone has a story worth sharing; we are just waiting for someone to listen."

—FRANK WARREN, author of *PostSecret*

I always cry when I chop onions.

My mom and I left my dad when I was 8. When I asked my dad how much he loved me he would always say "as much as all the onions in the world. Past, present and future."

I always cry when I chop onions.

INTRODUCTION

I've always been fascinated by the scale and complexity of the surrounding world and my place in it. Like most kids, I was awestruck by the unfathomable number of constellations in the night sky. As an adult, I watched people the same way I watched the stars. I kept wondering, what might we have in common with one another besides being strangers? I had a feeling the answers would be as beautiful as the constellations.

One morning, as I was sitting outside a coffee shop watching passersby, I got an idea. What if I just asked? I took my note book and a marker, and wrote:

I set the sign on the table and hoped that someone shared my curiosity. Within minutes, I got a response. Two women stopped and asked what I was doing. I told them I wasn't sure yet and invited them to write down

HI THERE! PLEASE STOP AND SHARE YOUR STORY!

anything about their lives. When they began to write, I knew my idea had weight; this might just work. Then more people stopped — lots of them. Strangers not only wanted to share their individual stories but were also seemingly relieved to do so. My burning curiosity to listen to people was met with their equally intense desire to be heard.

And so the Strangers Project was born. It's based on five basic principles:

1. People can write about anything they want as long as it's true
2. Stories are collected face-to-face in public spaces with a stack of blank paper, clip boards, and a lot of pens.
3. Stories are shared anonymously.
4. Stories must be spontaneously handwritten.
5. Everyone has a story.

Ten thousand entries and five years later, the Strangers Project is still going strong. This book is a curated selection of the strongest and most compelling entries from the collection, as well as photographs I've taken that show people reading and sharing stories.

While there's power in telling your own story, there is an equal bravery that comes with bearing witness to another's sorrows and joys. In this sense, "What's Your Story?" is an unusually active reading experience.

Though the stories are anonymous, each entry is a kind of self-portrait. Combined, they reveal the human condition.

These are the stories of the strangers we pass every day — people we don't know — and yet their hopes, dreams, and fears are as real as yours and mine.

Close your eyes: These strangers could be your friends, your family members, or your colleagues.

When I initially started this project, I wanted to create a physical and mobile space to give people the opportunity to be curious about their lives and the lives of others. What I've discovered is that the world needn't be so full of strangers. This project isn't just about reading and writing stories. It's about the connection that forms between storyteller and listener — and really, this connection is something we can explore every day in our own lives. It's about taking a moment of our day in which we give our time and undivided attention to one another. It's about acknowledging the people we share the world with and asking one simple question:

"WHAT'S YOUR STORY?"

— Brandon Doman

My first memory: Mom is waking me from a nap. The room is dark, mostly, but a wash of afternoon light spills in from the open door. "There's a surprise for you," Mom says, and points to a large cardboard box on the floor, right in the center of the room. A surprise? Ta-da! My best friend, ~~Sam~~, pops out of the box. Wonder and awe, but now I wouldn't know ~~him~~ if he were sitting right next to me.

Before that, or maybe a little after: I'm at the circus, clapping at the end of an act, and I look over at the kid next to me, who's also clapping. He smiles, then pushes me backward and I fall underneath the bleachers, underneath all the people, underneath everything it seems.

My first memories, but what came before? What's in the cardboard box? What's it like underneath the bleachers and the hollering crowd? I want to know. Or maybe I don't.

When I was six years old I fell. It wasn't a far drop off the railing of the wooden porch behind my house, only seven feet or so, but that height is so much greater when you're small. It was the first time the wind was knocked out of me, and I remember lying on my back, pain in my chest, unable to get the air back in my lungs, feeling that something terrible had happened and that, worst of all, my parents would never know, because I couldn't call to them. Of course, they had seen me fall from their vantage at the bay window, and came running to check on me. Their protection, to this day, is never far afield. But in those few moments before I knew they were coming, I was vulnerable, alone, and helpless.

I think of that memory today, I remember that feeling, and I wonder if it isn't a microcosm of childhood, one day believing being on tiptoe on the balance beam of a porch, the next, on your back unable to breathe. Perhaps a bit melodramatic, but I think of that a lot. How we become the people we are, and if we still are the people we were. How childhood is this precious, delicate thing, treasured and beautiful, but around every bend is something to knock us down. If we are lucky, we'll have parents to pick us up, but either way, we one day fall and see that seven feet isn't really that high, that we can survive that fall, even at the loss of the magic of ruling the world from a back porch.

—Washington Sq. Park on a perfect night

13

"The world is not
made out of atoms;
it is composed
of tiny stories"

— Muriel Rukeyser, author of *The Speed of Darkness*

In 2nd Grade, I thought I had found my Calling in Life; I wanted to be a ~~an~~ animal doctor (Thanks Ace Ventura) So when I found an injured squirrel while walking to a friends house, I thought God was saying "Here's your chance!" So I ran to my friend ~~[redacted]~~ house and told her to meet me with a box, and I ran home as fast as I could. I threw open the door and began tearing the house apart to find a suitable towel. My brother ~~[redacted]~~ chimed in over my shoulder, "what are you doing?" I responded "~~[redacted]~~ There's a squirrel! He's hurt! I'm going to help him!" ~~[redacted]~~ laughed, "Don't do it. Its gonna bite you!" I ran out the door. "No it wont! It will know I'm Helping it!" I met ~~[redacted]~~ ~~next~~ to the squirrell and she says "OK. Put it in the box." ~~[redacted]~~ I draped the towel over the squirrel and wrapped my hands around it. I slowly picked it up. Suddenly, the squirrel bit me through the towel. I dropped the ~~to~~ squirrel, furious he didnt ~~recognize~~ recognize I was try to help. ~~So~~ I ~~looked~~ down in fury to see the squirrel still attached to the towel. I picked up the towel, ~~to~~ whirled it around my head and snapped it (and the squirrel) against the tree. I ran home, my finger bleeding, sobbing screaming "I have rabies!" I threw open the door to find ~~[redacted]~~ in the living room. "He bite you?" ~~[redacted]~~ asked. I nodded. "Told you."

When I was younger, I've always wanted a pet zebra. That was only ~~scratch~~ a few years ago, when I was 7. Now I'm 11.

I asked my mom about ~~scratch~~ getting a pet zebra, and she said "NO ~~scratch~~ YOU CANNOT GET A PET ZEBRA DO YOU KNOW HOW ABSURD THAT IS?!" Maybe she wasn't actually yelling, but she wasn't like, ~~scratch~~ dear, we cannot get a pet zebra." So I decided to write a song about her called, "Dreamcrusher."

Now I know that the idea of getting a pet zebra is absurd, but then I ~~scratch~~ thought it was perfectly normal. I was a bit strange back then. When I was 4, I was a DEVIL CHILD!!! I bit my Pre-k teacher so many times. Seven years ago. But now I'm alright. I know that biting = BAD.

IS REMEMBERING A BLESSING
OR A CURSE?

I AM 61 YEARS OLD. MY LIFE HASN'T
BEEN MARRED BY MAJOR TRAGEDIES SUCH
AS WARFARE OR SERIOUS ILLNESS, BUT IT
HASN'T BEEN A COMFORTABLE EXPERIENCE,
EITHER. IT'S BEEN LIKE TAKING A LONG WALK
IN A PAIR OF SHOES THAT DIDN'T FIT— SOMEHOW
THE PERSONALITY AND THE DESTINY DIDN'T ALIGN.

FOR VARIOUS REASONS, MY LIFE NOW IS MORE DIFFICULT
THAN IT HAS EVER BEEN. THIS SOMEHOW DOESN'T
FEEL LIKE THE WAY IT SHOULD BE! ANYWAY, I OFTEN
FIND MY THOUGHTS TRAVELING BACK THROUGH TIME
TO THE 1970S AND 1980S, WHEN I WAS IN MY 20S AND 30S.
I REMEMBER HAPPY TIMES WITH FRIENDS NOW DEAD OR
DISPERSED, AND THE EXPERIENCE OF LIVING IN A PRE-
TERRORIST, PRE-TECHNOLOGICAL WORLD THAT WAS
MUCH SIMPLER AND MUCH MUCH LESS UPTIGHT. I REMEM-
BER WHAT MY BODY AND MY FACE AND MY SPIRIT WERE WHEN I WAS YOUNG.
SOMETIMES THE RECOLLECTIONS ARE COMFORTING,
AND SUMMONING UP THE LONG-AGO BRINGS A SMILE.
BUT AT OTHER TIMES, I HAVE TO TELL MYSELF,
"NO, NO, DON'T GO BACK, IT HURTS TOO MUCH" TO
REMEMBER BETTER DAYS. SO IS IT A BLESSING OR
A CURSE TO BE ABLE TO REMEMBER?

When I was three years old I scribbled on my kitchen's wallpaper with blue crayon. As time passed those was marks served as a moment of my childhood frozen in display, a glimpse of innocence where the rest escaped me. I grew up and my house was there to watch me when no one else would. In later years, my family tore the wallpaper off to replace with an annonymous shade of beige in preparation to sell the house, and I lost a capsule of who I was, with the blue marks discarded, recycled and forgotten. I look back on my 15 years living in my home as a phase passed, the foundation merely an exoskeleton and while its time for a new chapter in my definition of home, I will always miss that little blue scribble.

Hi,

I have been ~~ostracized~~ & bullied throughout my childhood. To relieve the burden of always being by myself when people didn't expect ~~you~~ me to be (~~lunch~~ cafeteria time for lunch, locker room before heading to the gym, etc.), I made up a fake friend who was all I ever hoped ~~to~~ a really cool friend would ~~be~~ and told everyone about him as if he was real. I lived my life with this imaginary friend for 10 years and I'm not sure whether I would've made it without him. Then, one day, I realized my life was no longer as vulnerable and I was stronger now. I had loving friends that I could rely on and I felt terrible about lying to them about this imaginary friend. So I killed him. I told everyone he died. ~~to a terrible~~ ~~car~~ I grieved as if he were real.

I knew it was a necessary thing to do, and I am proud of myself for moving on but I still feel a lot of guilt (10 years after I "killed" him) and I'm not sure whether the guilt is coming from having lied to people around me including my loved ones or ~~to~~ from having killed my (imaginary) friend. Isn't it weird? Even my husband doesn't know that this friend is not real, to this day. No one knows.

When I was a kid, on EASTER my parents got a rabbit. We were at my grandmothers house where I lived. It was a great Day and we had dinner then the adults went to the other Room to play cards.

Well, me and my brothers and sisters were watching TV and I was playing with the rabbit. I started holding the rabbit like a baby and throw him in the air, BUT then I missed and didn't catch him.

The rabbit wouldn't move. I didn't know what happened. I was too young to understand I had hurt it. I went to get my granfather who was an outdoorsman and knew about animals and was a dog breeder. the whole family gathered around the table. My grandad took out his glasses and examined the rabbit. Then he removed his glasses and said "Well that's it. He Killed it." Then my mother said - "He murdered it."

I am over 50 years old and I think about that almost everyday.

She is very special to me. And she happens to be beautiful as well. She is so... unique. When my mother or father leave me feeling alone or unappreciated, she comes to my side and stays with me as long as necessary. She just knows when I need her. She came into my life during a difficult time, and I've been fortunate to have her in my life for about 5 years now. Recently, I haven't been able to spend too much time with her. Granted, it's never enough. We've spent more time apart than together, but the time spent together is always precious and the memories everlasting. I have reached a new capacity for love, through her. I will always love her.

My dog's name is ~~Bella~~ and she is my best friend.

I was drawn to all things
teeny tiny when I was a kid.
My favorite book was the Wednesday Witch
by Ruth Chew. The witch makes a
magic scissors that shrinks stuff without
harming it. She shrinks her talking cat
who crawls into a dollhouse.
PARADISE: tiny + talking cat
I collected doll house furniture hoping
for a house one day. There were promises
and even a first floor of a mansion
begun. Life in my family was chaotic,
violent + unpredictable. Maybe I thought
if I could just make everything
small I would have more control.

You always have yourself. You are never alone. I remember a day in September so hot you could have cracked an egg on the blacktop and it would have fried. I was 8 years old and my jeans were torn↑ and stained from _from continuous falling_ the Georgia red clay that penetrated every corner of my school's playground. I had borrowed my friend's bike and had just spent the last two hours trying to teach myself how to ride a bike on my own. All my friends were experiencing the freedom bicycles offered. I wanted to taste that freedom. I wanted to feel the wind in my hair. The previous year whisked away my dad, the man whom would have taught me how to ride the frustrating bicycle...

hour #3, I felt the sweet success of accomplishing a goal on my own.

I had never owned an animal before, never had a pet until this past February. My fraternity's Alumni Advisor put on an alcohol awareness presentation and I showed up stoned. At the end, he explained that a woman he knew had a dog that was abandoned and needed rescuing. I volunteered. I named him ~~Otis~~ and never understood what ~~tot~~ unconditional love was until this little pitty came into my life. I'm a stoner, a frat boy, a failed son, unqualified to look after another, but I would do anything for him. I treat him like a small child and love him like one. He is just like his father too; his head a bit too big for his body, a whiner, a big hornball, but as loving and as affectionate as can be. 🐾

Every young man should have to raise a dog. It changes your outlook on life and the responsibility is a huge kick in the ass. In the college world of chasing pussy, getting cheated, boozin & slackin, a dog brings you back to Earth and says "Hey, snap the hell out of it and man up." Thank you, ~~Otis~~ I love you.

Cats. I love cats. At first I was a dog person, but as the years go by I really grew to love cats and how they lived their lives. Very mysterious and chill. Outdoor cats roam around all day and adventure the dangerous wilderness. Indoor cats sleep and take over your bed all day. I sometimes think it might be strange how much I like cats.... but hey whatever.

I always cry when I chop onions.

My mom and I left my dad when I was 8.
when I asked my dad how much he loved
me he would always say "as much as all
the onions in the world. Past, Present and future."

I always cry when I chop onions.

05.01.2013.

6/30/2014

To my mom,

Thank you, Thank you, Thank you.

You are by far my biggest supporter in life. You are my best friend, and an amazing person. Thank you for having my back when I wanted to leave home for the BIG CITY, and once again when I chose to study in London. Not once have I ever felt a sense of doubt from you. You truely and honestly have shaped me into the strong, independent, talkative woman I am. Much of which is reflected in you.

Thank you for loving me when I've been a bitch, because we both know thats often. You blame it on the city, but I know it's because I dont spend enough time with you. Lastly, thank you for never ever judging. You have always made me feel worthy, even when I was 30 lbs heavier, when I couldnt make friends in college, and when I lost my virginity after a first date. Just one of my many bad decisions you smoothed over. I can never imagine loving another person more then you, not just emotholly, but just bve for your spirit. You are an amazing woman. You are a beautiful person. You are a perfect mother. I will always love you more.

XOXO Your sunshine girl

I used to live on L.I. Now I live in Thousand Oaks, CA. I'm back in NY for the unveiling of my dad's memorial stone at the cemetary. Now I'm turning 60 & very sad I no longer have parents. I know some people lose their parents much earlier, but I still feel the loss.

I wish I had been nicer to my parents. I didn't realize it would end so abruptly. Saturdays come & I go to call my mom, then I remember. No mom. You can have many friends & relatives but there is nothing in life like your mom.

I was about 2 when I first saw him. What was I supposed to think? He's a boy, I'm a girl. I don't even know if I knew what it meant to be another human being with different feels and a different story. I guess you could say we grew up together. He always sort seemed to be... there. When we were 6 he lost his first tooth. His mouth gushed blood. He was terrified and I fell over laughing. ~~He~~ cried and screamed for his mom. Between my tears of laughter I saw his scared deep blue eyes. He pleaded, begging for some kind of help. I didn't know what to do so I grabbed a strawberry and threw it into my mouth, smooshing the juices around until a thick red juice trickled down my chin. I guess you could say we looked ~~ridiculous~~ ridiculous. but his tears dried and he stared at me for a while. His eyes wide with wonder. The red juice dripped and ~~stained~~ my pink princess dress. He let out a big laugh and I could see a big gap between his teeth. It looked red and ~~swollen~~ swollen and puffy. His mouth closed and he looked at me again. My heart jumped. That's when I knew I was in love with a toothless blue eyed goof.

I have a brother with severe cerebral palsy.
When I was really young, ~~xx~~ I shared everything
with him. Then during my teenage years & with the
onset of excruciating self-consciousness, I got really
embarrassed of his disability. He only has control from
his neck upwards, so his ~~body~~ regularly goes into
spasm, ~~communicate~~ He ~~communicates~~ through his eyes
& through the dedication of my mother, a communication
system has been set-up, all achieved through the
direction his eyes point in. He is an exceptionally
bright person (now ~~stat~~ undertaking a degree) &
a hugely charismatic guy.
Looking back, I regret those years I felt embarrassed
- what he ~~cook~~ has achieved & how he has taught
me to make the most of every moment given to
you is hugely humbling. He's an incredible person
with a wicked sense of humour & I just want
to sing his praises all the time now.

I used to think I was really ugly. And I think Everyone Does at some point... unless you're -Beyoncé- ... but then I realized my problems were kinda small. My younger sister was diagnosed with depression. She told me she felt ugly. She told me her thoughts felt ugly. So one day she told me "YOU ARE SO BEAUTIFUL!" and I figured if she could muster up that wonderful thought from the depths of all her dangerous ones then maybe I really was beautiful and maybe SHE was really beautiful. I know this maybe is a little cliché, the tale of a girl who thought she was ugly, but then realized she was gorgeous, but it's really more of an observation about the way we come to understand the beauty in others. That between the horrors of suicidal thoughts and life breaking depression there are specks of grace that are so gripping, they're almost tangible. So guess what? My sister is beautiful and so am I.

7 years ago, my mother was diagnosed with schizophrenia.
She would laugh hysterically in the middle of the night and accuse people
of plotting to murder her. She would rehearse her parents. She stopped
raising me. I was in 6th grade with a brother in 1st grade. My father
worked every day to support us, but home became hell.
 I felt betrayed by a woman who was supposed to be strong, supportive,
and my hero. And I hated her.
For years, I've forgotten the good things she did, the way she raised me
into who I am, the way she influenced my life.
She didn't come to NYU for my ~~first day~~ moving in to my freshman
dorm. She didn't say goodbye when I moved ~~of~~ out.
 But I've learned to look beyond her illness, and respect who she was.

I'm a 20 year old university student in Leeds, United Kingdom. I'm originally from there, but I moved to Spain when I was 9 and returned to England when I was 18. My time in Spain was hard, my dad turned to cocaine and alcohol, and living out of his car instead of being home with his family. I used to clean out his car when he'd come home (rare, but it happened sometimes) and I'd have to empty litre bottles of urine into the gutters and take him to bed. Despite our family falling apart, my mother kept me sane, and this trip to NYC is the reason why I know that no matter what, my mother will always be the rock in my life. My dad paid nothing since I left, yet she worked everyday, all year, to ensure I had a future. This trip, is 2 years worth of work and salary, just so she could make me happy.

I love her.

My mother's sister died at the age of 17 from a sudden brain aneurysm. I never got the chance to meet her, but the age difference between her and my mom was the same as the one between me and my sister. She was the younger sister. I'm the younger sister. My mother doesn't talk about her often, but when she does, she always says I remind her of her little sister. She's been telling me that since I was a little girl and when I was younger, it made me think I was walking down the same path she was. I knew it was crazy, but a part of me thought growing up that I, too, would not make it past the age of 17. (I'm 23 now, so needless to say everything went fine.) But it's a strange feeling living in the shadow of someone you never met. I feel a connection with her and sometimes I feel like she's watching me. And every day I make it past the age of 17, I live not only for myself, but for her too.

When I was 4 years old I was building the Barbie Dream House that I got from Santa... the next thing I remember was my mom running into her bedroom and my dad telling my older sister, 9, to call 911. The next thing I remember was my mom being carried out on a stretcher. She died two weeks later. It was an aneurism. I'm 19 years old now and that is the earliest memory I have. Even though it's sad, I choose never to forget it. Since my mom died, I watched my dad battle alcoholism and depression. I still can't imagine ever being in his shoes. Sure I lost my mom, but he lost the love of his life. I think that many people would choose to be bitter and angry and upset but I learned early on from this that life stops for no one. If I decided to be all of those things after my mom died, I would be wasting my time. I will never know if I am the way I am because my mom died or if it's just who I'm meant to be. But I honestly believe that some mysterious power had control that day. And I am okay with that. By sharing my story with other people I have realized that it's helped other people open up about their stories and emotions. And when I tell people my story, they seem to be shocked because I'm such a smiley positive person. I don't put up a fake wall but I'm positive because I know no other way. I love cheesy inspirational quotes. I love a warm cup of coffee. I love vanilla cupcakes with vanilla buttercream frosting. I love a vase of fresh flowers. I love photographs. I love knowing how small I am in the world because there's so much left to see. I love the smile on people's faces when they are passionate about something. I just love to love. Loving is so much more powerful than being angry about life. So just love more. Take the opportunity to notice the ordinary things in life, not just big moments. There's so much power in the little things in life. So try all that life has to offer, because life stops for no one.

XOXO

I feel like every day I'm this little girl walking around the room with her mom's stilletos. I know how things are supposed to work but I can't quite achieve it. And it's eating me alive. I yearn for a release, to get rid of the strings pulling me back. But the thing is, I'm holding them. So tight. So tight it burns my hands. But I'm so used to the ache that I'm not sure how to live without it. People don't see the strings, they think I'm free. People think a lot of things about me that are not true, because I'm breathing lies. I'm a very honest person, with a very selective honesty. And I'm so full of ideals but all I think about is how much I want someone to share them with. I don't. I never do. If I stop and reflect over it, I feel so incredibly meaningless that survival seems like the hardest of tasks. You might have noticed that my brain is really scattered, a billion thoughts fight for their spot on the podium. I want you to know you're special. If you're reading this (still, after all the blabbering), whoever you are and whereever, you're sharing a moment no one else is experiencing right now. Just you and I. Maybe we'd be good friends. I'm a vegetarian though, so we probably wouldn't be sharing ribs in front of the TV. But ice cream would work. I like ice cream. A lot. (too much?). Anyway. I'm running around in circles. I don't like writing on the spot. It takes me 5 readings, usually, until I'm satisfied with the essence and the wording of something I write.

Sometimes I wonder if my problems are my parents' fault. My mom is uptight. My dad is silent. They never quite understood me, and I doubt they ever will. It's hard though, understanding another human being. I wonder why people assume sharing blood would make it easier. It doesn't. We're still all a mystery except to ourselves. And it's hard accepting that we're all alone. But we are. People are around us, and I believe in intense connections, but... we are alone. I think I understood that too early. My thoughts are a virus that has taken over every cell in my body. I truly wish I could be free of them, and I will be eventually when my body grows rigid, but it's a full-time job with no vacation. But it's true that if you love what you do, you'll never work a day in your life. So we have to accept it. Embrace it. Love it. Because we are our own first and last love.

This is so bad. I have so much to say.
But if we meet someday,
I promise we'll like each other,
And maybe you'll understand.
And maybe I'll like you enough I'll eat ribs in front of the TV.
Just kidding!

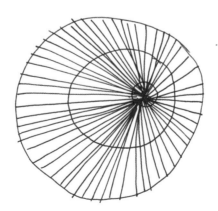

Before we part, let me ask you a question, do you ever allow yourself to be fully vulnerable?
I try. But it's my biggest failure.

I am an only child. I have always been alone.
As a child I delved into my imagination all the time
and had a hard time enjoying reality. I never had
any imaginary friends and had a hard time making
friends in general. I did talk to myself A LOT, had
some very fascanating conversations with myself. I still
talk to myself and actually prefer to be alone.

I am a very independant person and enjoy having
adventures by myself. I don't have any close friends
but enjoy meeting people as aquantances only.
I just don't have the skills it takes to make
a true connection with people, only temporary ones.
I get claustrophic easily.

I ask myself sometimes, is this because
I'm an only child? Or is there something wrong

with me?

When I was six, I once drowned a kitten in the canal beneath my house. I still remember its mewling as it was carried away by the current, the rolling thunder as it tried to drown out my sin.

It was not an act of cruelty, though it was definitely cruel in its effect. I had found the kitten beneath a car, and in my six-year old mind thought it abandoned. I grabbed it, brought it home, and then realizing that there was no way my parents would let me keep it, brought it downstairs. I placed it on a dish, and poured milk onto its feet. It refused to drink. It wouldn't stop mewling, probably for its own mother. I picked it up. I still remember the stickiness of its fur, plastered across its legs. I was angry.

I brought it to the area near the canal. It was storming. The kitten wouldn't stop mewling. I felt a rage gather in my throat. Clumsy fingers tried to clamp the kitten's mouth shut. They couldn't.

I pushed the kitten off, and watched it get carried away by the current. Then, I went to go have dinner. I didn't think anymore of this. But somehow, to this day, I remember every single detail of that day, and I have never forgiven myself for it. I can't forget those last cries, sharp in the pattering of rain, as they disappeared into the rushing waters.

I have a fiance now. We will be married soon. And I am terrified, of my clumsy fingers, of another irrational mistake made in anger. But I am older now. And I have this story.

I am sorry, kitten, wherever you are. I took away what I had no right to. Please forgive me.

Please forgive me.

My dad was never really a great father and I never remember feeling a connection or loving him. Then in 3rd grade, my parents divorced and I never saw my Dad again. For a long time, I was envious of other girls who had amazing fathers + could share their journey through life with. I never wished my dad was back in the picture, but I felt slighted that I wasn't born with a great dad. Then as I got older + met more people from different walks of life, I realized how extremely <u>lucky</u> I was to have a really amazing mother. Someone who loved me unconditionally, was my biggest supporter + motivator, attended every game I ever played in and every award ceremony I ever had. She worked so extremely hard as a single mother to be the best and make sure I had every opportunity that she didn't. She paid for me to go to college + move to NYC. So now as I'm almost 30, I realize that I wasn't slighted, I am <u>extremely</u> blessed to have <u>one</u> amazing parent because so many people don't.

As I walk about the city of my childhood I keep thinking/ hoping/dreading (?) that I might cross paths with my homeless father. He doesn't know I'm here – I didn't tell him. The only reason, or the biggest reason is because I am here with my mother and I don't want her to make me seeing him about herself. I'd like to get him an annual gym membership so he has a place to shower, hit on girls in their early 20's (maybe he'll read their astrology chart and get to crash on their couch a few nights), play squash...whatever. If I gave him cash he'd probably day trade it away or lose it in some pyramid scheme.

Anyhow, when I was a toddler, I'd skinny dip in the fountain here at Washington square park... some of my earliest and fondest memories were made here. A particularly formative one – I saw a live bumblebee being ravaged by ants. My child mind questioned... should I let nature take it's course? Stomp the bee and innocent ants? Put the bee to die in the calyx of a flower? Ohhhhh.... Service & caretaking ~ a joy, a struggle!

All my life I had been confused about ~~who~~ who I was, what I was going to do and where I was going to be in the future. I come from a family with a rich military history. We can trace our military roots back to the civil war. My great grand father was a Tuskegee Airman, my grand father served in Korea, my father in Vietnam. My mother was a marine, my uncle served in the Army. So in order to find myself I felt that I had to serve.

I have always been confused about my gender. I thought that serving would confirm that I was male. I went to Valley Forge Military Academy and slowly learned that I was not male. I became depressed and suicidal but was too much of a coward to take my own life. But I continued on with my plan to serve but with a purpose. I was going to find the most dangerous job that I could and hope that it would kill me. I joined the Navy and volunteered for E.O.D. (Explosive Ordinance Disposal). This, I was sure, would kill me. The first Iraq conflict arose and I volunteered for detatched duty with an Army Ranger unit tasked to defuse I E D's. Much to my chagrin I became good friends with everyone in the squad and felt that I had to do my job well. I was the best at what I did.

On one patrol we came under fire and we were pinned down with little ammo left. The enemy rushed our position and I dove in front of one squad mate to shield him from fire. I took 2 rounds in the back. My vest stopped one round the other got through. I felt the blackness taking me and thought to myself mission accomplished. I woke in the infirmary and this saddened me. But the one good thing that came out of it was that male or female, I knew that it was not my time to go. I had to realize who I was. Years later I have started to transition to female knowing that this story, among many other helped me find myself. My stories of my journey will help others who are searching for themselves. I as a person have valee and I am meant to be a guide to others.

I was eight years old. It was November 19th, 2003.
I remember the date well. My sister and I had
been staying with my father in Georgia while
my mother was in another state pursuing other
~~interests~~. occupational interests. Halloween had
just passed and from the worldview of an eight
year old girl, life was beautiful and nothing short
of idyllic. ~~Everyone was happy~~

Day after day passed, ~~building memories of that~~
each seeming even more joyous than the previous
until one day he started collapsing. ~~This allow~~ Within
hours he went from ~~collapsing~~ taking care of his two
daughters to being taken care of by his two daughters
while unconscious. ~~Despite all attempts~~

I didn't understand death. I felt cheated, alone, and
most of all I felt like an adult.

I MISS HER. SHE WAS MY HERO AND I DON'T KNOW IF I EVER TOLD HER THAT; AND IF I DID, I DON'T KNOW IF I EVER TOLD HER ENOUGH.

SHE PASSED AWAY ALMOST THREE MONTHS AGO, AND NOW SHE IS NOWHERE AND EVERYWHERE AT THE SAME TIME.

I'M SURE SHE LEFT ME WITH EVERYTHING I NEED, ~~FIERCELY~~ FIERCELY INDEPENDENT SHE MADE ME; ~~AND I DON'T EVEN~~ I TRIED TO SHOW HER THAT SHE HAS EQUIPPED ME TO LOOK AFTER MYSELF, TO THE POINT THAT I'D NEVER GO TO HER WITH PROBLEMS. I HOPE SHE NEVER FELT LIKE I DIDN'T NEED HER. AND NOW, I CAN'T EVEN GO TO HER IF I WANTED TO. WHO AM I SUPPOSED TO GET GUYS APPROVED BY? WHO AM I SUPPOSED TO ASK IF I SHOULD VACCINATE MY KIDS? OR AT WHAT TEMPERATURE I'M SUPPOSED TO COOK HER FAMOUS CHICKEN IN?

IF YOU STILL HAVE YOUR MOTHER, ~~PLEASE~~ CALL HER. SQUEEZE HER NO MATTER HOW SMALL SHE MAY BE. MAKE ~~█~~ SHE _KNOWS_ THAT YOU LOVE HER, AND IF YOU'RE IN DOUBT ABOUT IT START WORKING ON IT, BECAUSE THIS IS ONE REGRET YOU NEVER WANT TO HAVE IN LIFE — NOT BEING SURE THAT ~~YOU BED~~ YOUR MOTHER ~~KNOW~~ _KNEW_ THAT YOU LOVED HER.

Sept. 5TH 2014

I HAVE A POOR SENSE OF TIME.

Not the literal, everyday practical use of time, but rather, the concept of it being applied. I see my grandmother, 91 years old with still, a head half covered in black hair. The greys seem to be kept at bay by her strong will and sharp mind.

But she will die soon. Soon, being that period of upcoming days of which in the near future, I will be acutely aware of It, almost without any warning. But I will know, because I have watched her age for twenty - three years. But there is no urgency, her d.

↑
BULLSHIT

TL;DR - MY MOM DIED WHEN I WAS SEVEN.
SO WHY DOES IT FEEL LIKE EVERYONE
I KNOW WILL LIVE FOREVER?

AND WHEN THEY DIE, WHY DO I GET THE FEELING
I WON'T MISS THEM?

it's terrifying.

She spent her last hours
of consciousness comforting us,
telling us that she was okay,
that it didn't hurt, and that
we would be fine without her.

I never knew how strong someone could be until I watched my mom die. I'd known it was coming, she had been diagnosed with stage 4 ovarian cancer 3 years before, but I still didn't feel ready. I was 28, had been on my own for years, but still couldn't picture life without my mom. In the year since she's passed I realize how brave and strong she was, especially in those final days. Most people, including me, would have been angry at what they were facing, the pain, both physical and emotional of losing your life and missing out on your children and grandchildren's futures, but not mom. She spent her last hours of consciousness comforting us, telling us that she was okay, that it didn't hurt, and that we would be fine without her. And she was right, surprisingly, we are all doing okay. We miss her every day but life does go on and she wouldn't want us to miss it on her account (she told us so all the time — along with trying to convince dad it would be okay if he married the woman who cut his hair that she was convinced hit on him every time they went there). I hope she knows we're happy and okay (and that dad has no intention of marrying his hair cutter). Love you mom!

2 WEEKS FROM NOW, I'M ON THE FIRST ~~STEPS~~
STEPS FROM HELPING THE ONE PERSON THAT
MADE ME SMILE, LAUGH + CRY ~~FOR~~ MORE THAN
ANY LOVER EVER HAS.

July 8, 2014, I'M GOING TO HAVE A ~~Blood~~
Blood TEST THAT COULD DECIDE IF ~~ANY~~
MY MOM WILL GET A NEW (slightly & USED)
~~K~~ ~~@~~ KIDNEY. TO DECIDE THIS TOOK
LAUGHTER, ~~TER~~ TEARS + A DEAL WITH GOD,
~~Bodha~~ Buddha + ~~THI~~ THE UNIVERSE.
TO SEE HER HAPPY IS #1, TO SEE
HER OUT OF THE HOUSE + OFF THE
~~PLASTIC~~ MACHINE THAT KEEPS HER ALIVE.
WHILE SHE IS ON THE MACHINE, I DON'T
SLEEP ~~ALL~~ AT NIGHT, NAPS ARE THE ~~ANY~~ TIMES
MY BRAIN SHUTS DOWN.

I'M ~~SCAR~~ SCARED + ~~YET~~ YET HOPEFULLY
SHE WILL GET BETTER.
    I JUST WANT TO SEE HER NOT
CONNECTED TO THE MACHINE !!
        WISH ~~MY~~ ME LUCK. !!

Today I recieved an
email that they found
a match in the bone marrow
drive I ran this past sumer.
I helped save a life!
You can too!! :)

Just smile

Today is Beautiful ♥

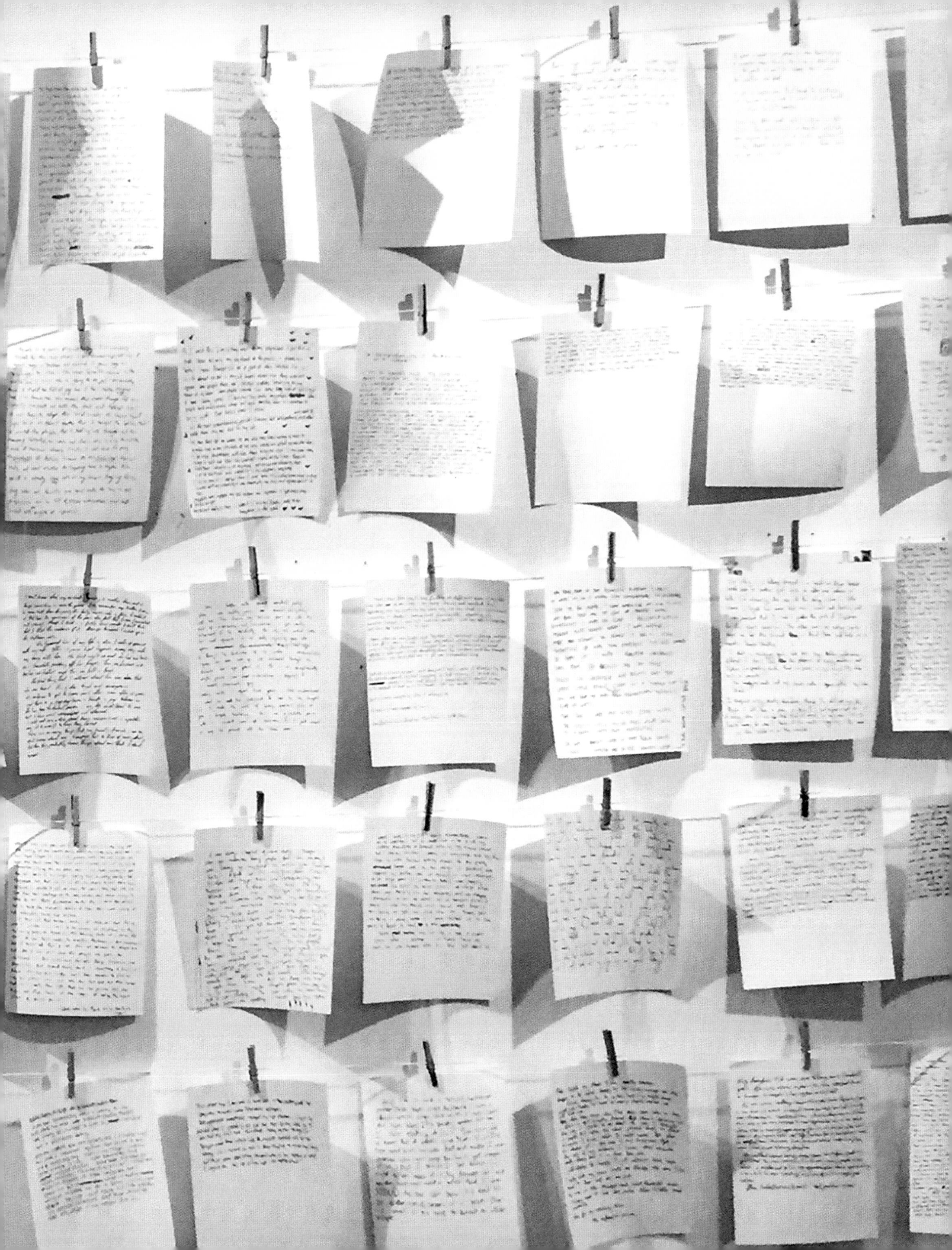

When I am on the subway or the metro or whatever you call it in your city, I watch others. I imagine their lives and I hope for the best. I think of the strength I am (statistically) surrounded by at any moment: people who have survived cancer, people who sacrifice for their children or mothers every day; people who come out despite the odds; people who love and have sex after surviving sexual assault; people who work hard, exhausting, back breaking jobs for their family; people who keep going.

Thank you for letting me imagine your story and glimpse your strength.

I wake up and I smile. But I do cry. We all do. We all have our struggles we all have our demons, we all have a battle. Last week my Aorta bleed out on the operating table, And Im alive. My surgery didn't go as planned, but Im still here and thats what matters. I still have Cancer, I still have this disease but the important thing is I have my life. I have my family & my friends. and I have never been more appreciative of that in my entire life. I just want to say keep fighting for those out there that are struggling. I know its hard but I promise you itl be okay.

☺ -Smile

June 2013

I was recently diagnosed with leukemia. ~~a~~ It's been pretty rough dealing with school, work, relationships and treatment! It really sucks being diagnosed so young (19) I know its not that young of an age but it still sucks. The only person who makes me happy these days is my girlfriend. She doesn't make me feel like a cancer patient or that i'm going to die tomorrow. This woman makes me feel alive and I absolutely love her for it. Unfortunately she isn't a NYC native. (she lives in D.C) But I swear if I beat ~~it~~ my diagnosis, and if she'll have me, i'll marry her.

many people are scared of dying, but I'm not one of them. I'm the opposite. I'm scared of never really living. I want to do so much with my life that I get overwhelmed thinking about how I will do it all and then I begin to think about the chance I won't do any of it. The one thing I want to ~~do have~~ feel before I pass on into whatever happens after death is I want to feel wanted. When I write it down it sounds lame & selfish, but then I realize it is because I am not articulating what <u>want</u> means. I want to have this unbelievable connection with someone else that after meeting each other all each of us can do is think about how much we want, no need the other person. That to me is living. Feeling so much passion & connection with someone else that you feel the waves of energy between you two. That ability to feel that is ~~what~~ what I fear of never having. The worst part about this fear is I can't do anything to make it happen. I just have to wait.

This summer, I found out that the person that I have been calling "Daddy" all my life, is not my biological father. And the way I found out... was like a scene that existed in TV shows or movies. It was dramatic, sudden, and life changing.

My aunt had gotten into a huge fight with her husband. My mom, wanting to get my aunt back with my uncle and her children, tried persuading her to calm down. Instead, it backfired. My aunt felt that my mom had betrayed her and in return, spilled the biggest secret that my mom had: I was a result of her and her ex-boyfriend. How did I know all this? I was woken by my aunt's screaming at 3am in the morning. However, I pretended to be fast asleep so no one knows I know the secret.

I have never been particularly close with my dad. I used to always look at other daughters with their dads on the street and feel an immense amount of jealousy ~~of~~ their closeness and intimacy.

Now, all I feel is profound thankfulness and happiness that my dad is my dad.

~~Because~~ It's not the people who give birth to you that are great. It's the people who watch you grow and nurture you that are the greatest.

When you raise a child in a home filled with abuse and hate, you are responsible for setting them up for a life of pain and lovelessness.

I used to tell myself that. And I still fundamentally believe it. It's mom's fault, why I have violent tendencies and zero self-esteem. It's dad's fault, for hitting me and cheating on mom. I am a failure as a daughter, friend, social being, lover, and it's my parents fault for raising me that way.

At some point, though, I have to assume control of who I am and how I treat others.

IT'S NOT YOUR FAULT

BUT IT'S YOUR PROBLEM.

I can, and you can, choose to be more than your upbringing. More than what people told you to be, or shaped you to be. The best revenge I can achieve, is to live a happy life, and to actively spread happiness in the world, As often as I can.

It's hard to change your nature.

It's hard to teach yourself how to love others, when you never really were taught.

It's hard to assume responsibility when your childhood left you feeling powerless and weak.

BUT you have to do it. I have to do it. Because otherwise, I am nothing more than a product of hate. I choose to break the cycle of hate and helplessness.

I am here in NYC to visit an oncologist for a second opinion on my post-surgery options for my breast cancer. I have DCIS (ductile carcinoma in situ). I don't want to be known for my breast cancer. I AM NOT MY BREAST CANCER.

I am a mother, a wife, a sister, a daughter, a cityphile, a lover, a friend, a locavore foodie cook, a progressive, a person of non-violence, and so much more. That's what I want to be seen as — a human being.

And today I am a mother, here with my teen daughter enjoying our time together, like watching the bird walking under my seat. I am going to stay in the present, and not worry about tomorrow.

I AM NOT
MY BREAST CANCER.

July 5, 2014

One month ago today, my mom passed away from stomach cancer. It's still so hard to believe.

I see the model of her car driving down the road and eagerly search the driver's side, hoping to see her face. Only then will I exhale.

As a social worker, I have heard how fucked up parents can be and have seen what this does to a child. I could have been born with a crazy mother, but instead, I was blessed with one that taught me to never give up and to value education. I miss her so much. I miss her mispronanciation of words, her hands, her calling me "monkey"... yet I feel like my mom has prepared me for this moment. Growing up she always told us "You need to learn how to do this because one day I won't be here" AND HERE I AM. Master's degree, LSW... I owe it all to her!

This week was a better week but from what I hear the longer the time the worse it gets. There's a hole in my heart but never have I felt as much love in my entire life as in this past month. My family has come together in a way that we never have (I hope that doesn't change!) and I have fallen in love with a man, THEE MAN ☺ He came at a time where I wasn't looking for anything b/c I was focused on taking care of my mom. In the 2 months before she passed he was able to build a relationship w/ her. He was able to call her MOM ☺ One day I will never forget took place at the hospital. The cancer had spread to her brain and at this point she was mostly non-verbal. She was somehow able to gather the strength to put his hand together with mine. I am convinced that she gave us her blessing. Today, I am continuing her fight by warning others of the dangers of conventional medicine—chemo & radiation and am asking others to look further into holistic alternative tx before resorting to other extremes. I can only hope that this message falls into the right hands.
                                                                        STAY STRONG ♡

64

I'm currently sitting in a park that's been as much a part of my life, as much as it has been a part of my mom's life. I used to work at the university that surrounds this park, and 20 years earlier, I was a freshman at this university. Many years before that, my mom went to the same university for her Masters' degree. And some time after that, she gave birth to me at the medical center run by this university. I should probably be bleeding the university's color — purple — which happens to be my mom's favorite color.

Nearly 5 years ago, I moved back to this city to start a new job at this university... and to be with my mom, who was battling cancer again. Two weeks after I moved back, she died. And I wasn't there, despite my best efforts to get there — to her bedside — quickly. Suddenly, the only reason I moved back ceased to be, and I had to find a way to move on and build — or rebuild — a new life, just to fill the void. After 2 years, I felt comfortable enough to write a song to immortalize her and ~~the~~ effect her passing ~~on me~~ had on me. I felt comfortable enough to sing again. I felt comfortable enough to try things I've never done before, so I can live my life to the fullest — just like my mom did right before she started battling cancer for the second time. And I seem to be wearing a lot more purple while I do it.

I am surviving brain cancer. So far.

Title: Our Present

~~Five and ½ years ago, 3 days before~~

Three days before we were married, 5½ years ago I found that I had prostate cancer. My soulmate married me anyway. Since then we have been fighting the cancer and living an amazing life, where each day we get to peak behind the curtain at the never ending wonders of precious life.

Recently we have learned that the cancer is winning. I have begun experimental treatments with the hope of keeping the inevitable at bay. As I sit in the park writing this story, I search for words for you, my reader, to understand how grateful we should all be to be a part of this amazing universe, this ~~dirty~~ never ending present which is always accessible whenever we are brave enough to open our eyes.

As to how this story ends... it doesn't. My love and I are part of this universe, as is time.... and we will be with the present forever. And since as we have we met, we will continue to thank God and the universe for every present we share.

My handwriting is terrible b/c I
am a new lefty. I had Spinal Surgery
a year ago to have a tumor removed
from my spine. I was wheelchair bound
for 2 wks and lost the feeling in
my right hand. It's gotten enormously
better but it's still not 100%. But
that's ok! I'm really proud of myself.
I still live in NYC and book
frequent acting gigs. Go me!
If I can conquor that, I can
conquor anything!

XO

I'm 22 years old. I'm from England. I'm currently sat writing this in Washington Square Park, New York. I'm sat next to my beautiful girlfriend. After reading some of the entries in The Strangers Project I have mixed emotions. I've never been divorced. I've never had a life threatening disease. I've never really been in a position of true struggle. I guess I'm lucky. I should be more appreciative. I need to be more thankful for what I have. Maybe I won't be this lucky forever. I really don't know how my future will pan out. I feel like I should really have a better plan. So I guess I don't truely know my story. Maybe thats ok. I'm going to try and enjoy the NOW alot more. I'm lucky. I have my health. I have my family and friends. I have this amazing girl sat next to me. I love her. I know there will be obstacles to overcome. But I hope by the end I will look at my life as one great story.

When I was 16, all I wanted was a pair of knee-high, lace-up Dr. Marten boots. Instead, I got pregnant. Priorities changed, and while I sometimes looked wistfully at the Docs in the windows of shops while back-to-school shopping for my son, I had no regrets that life as a single mom working for a non-profit made $150 boots far out of my league.

When my son was 18, he took the proceeds from his first paycheck to buy me my best Christmas present ever— a pair of knee-high lace-up Dr. Martens. For four years I have walked the world with the soul of my son on my feet.

When he was 20, he told me he was ready to move out. Instead, I left him with the house and the dogs in Colorado and moved to New York City with 2 suitcases and a backpack to start my Act 2.

Life in NY is giddy, gleeful bliss! Having raised an entire, wonderful person, there's no pressure to be anything but who I am. For the first time, life is 100% on my terms. Freedom is a ridiculous privilege and everyday is well earned joy— 40 truly couldn't be better. Now I can focus just on my mission — to empower people to realize their full potential + make the world a better place. And every day is better than the last...

Struggles of A Mother

I have 2 boys I raised alone.
Living in the Projects It's hard to keep Kid's
from getting Involved in all the Street nonsense.
I decided to dedicate my life to my Kids.
I put them to play Baseball with Kids Against
Drugs Baseball. My son which is Now 19
Started playing at the age of 6 with the
league. While in his teens Mom would go
where ever she needed and spend her last
Penny in order for her Kids to have what they
needed. needless to say she had No personal
Life since her boys were her life. At this
present time My Son is Now 19 yrs of age
and is still playing baseball For collage.
Plus he umpires for the league that helped
him learn the Sport. My 2nd son is on
his way to Collage he is a senior in High school.
I did it all alone, and I can say I'M
Proud to be the Mom of 2 Men No
Longer boys.

Oct. 25th, 2013

The decision to give up on a career was not easy for me. I chose to get married, and for us, two people in school at once was not an option. I graduated from college with a bachelor's degree shortly before our wedding and have been working as a receptionist ever since. I have felt this incredible pull to go back to school, start a career, be the person _everyone_ expected me to be. My whole life I have been expected to be amazing, and the second I realized I might not be living up to that, I felt that pull stronger than I ever had before. Now don't get me wrong, I love my husband and I have a very happy marriage. But I was constantly wondering if I was squelching my potential. Well, I just found out I'M PREGNANT... For me, this means I probably wont ever have the career I dreamed of. But for the first time, _ever_, I feel like I have the opportunity to become who I want to be. I can live up to _my_ expectations. It was immediate. This feeling of love, of happiness, of fear, of everything. I now can honestly say I am ok with where I am at in my life. I am going to be a MOTHER. I love that title and I feel so honored to have it.

The day my daughter was born was one of the worst days of my life. I had dreamed of that day for so long. I imagined the triumphant + beautiful moment when she would be placed on my chest. It would be a spiritual peak of my life.

But that moment never happened. My body failed us both. She was born at 29 weeks by cesarian. She weighed less that 2 lbs. she was put on a respirator in an incubator. - far from my arms in a NICU.

She's a beautiful + healthy 18 year old starting college in Manhattan. She's a treasure in my life. But I'll always feel ripped off that we didn't get a beautiful "hello."

my mom found my pot cookies and ate one. I was at work and I got a text saying, "I found these cookies in the back of your closet, can I have one?" Asking as if finding a plate of cookies underneath a pile of sweaters was totally normal. Anyways, she didn't even wait for my response and she ate one. I came home after work and she was hysterically laughing at Armageddon, with my dad shaking his head while seated in his chair. I did eventually find out she took more cookies for herself late.

Cool mom.

FOR MY MOTHER:

I'm afraid to write this knowing you'll recognize my handwriting but maybe that's not such a bad thing. Last weekend you came to visit and I loved seeing you here. As we both know, I hate coming home. I think you took that personally. You shouldn't have. But last weekend ~~it~~ it meant so much to see you partly because I miss you (I know you don't believe me but I do) and partly because I thought I was pregnant.

~~Past~~ the initial knee-jerk reaction of 18 and pregnant alone in New York City, we fell in love with our baby. I'm sure you want to know how he reacted— you'd love him for it. He was so supportive. We decided on abortion on the first night but it would be a few days before we could confirm/get the abortion and in those few days we fell in love with the baby. We named it ~~Isla~~ if it was a girl, ~~Isaac~~ ~~Ezra~~ if it was a boy. But we ~~Isla~~ weren't sure about ~~Isaac~~ ~~Ezra~~ after my ~~Dad~~. As you probably guessed, I'm not pregnant. And that's good but I miss the baby I'm not having. So does he. I keep wondering if you noticed my hand on my stomach all weekend. I wanted to tell you so badly but I knew you wouldn't take it well after your similar history. Well that's not true. I knew you would take it well. I guess I just didn't want to remind you. I wanted to emulate your strength. I wonder if I'll ever tell you about it. I doubt it. I love you. An if it got too melodramatic I have to stop before I turn on My Chemical Romance and revert back to my 15 yr old self. Bye Mom

I had my first baby 7 weeks ago. she's beautiful +
so sweet + calm like her papa. It's been a
huge emotional rollercoaster for me + her dad.
we've been fooling around or living together or
married for 23 years and I'm 35 now so most of
my life. we've also been friends + not friends +
~~musical partners~~ bandmates + not in a band + now
we have become one in this little baby. I thought
everything was a fairy tale + was very happy in the
days after her birth but daddy was really going
through something else. He was reflecty on years +
years of emotion, anger, resentment, sadness
about being in a relationship with me. It came
as ~~a~~ a shock hearing all this emotion exploding
out of him all at once, things I had never heard +
things I never want to hear. This tiny baby has
super powers! She can transform time + shake
you up! I think for our future, ~~all~~ all of
us, baby too, it will be good that daddy brought
up the things that are hurting him, so thank you
little baby for transforming us. We both love you
with our whole hearts, minds, bodies + with the
promise of our whole lives. Life is not a fairy
tale (duh!) but you are loved by people with
tremendous capacity to love + communicate . xoxo

I'm walking around Art Fair by myself, looking at all the families, mothers with their children, fathers tugging toddlers along the tired road. I immediately feel this "pang" in my heart that's so familiar. a longing for a family... and then, I smile. after those 12 years of trying to conceive my two little boys are at home with their dad.. and I have an hour at Art Fair by myself... to people watch.

My wife is 9 weeks pregnant today! I'm incredibly excited for this next phase in our relationship. We met 8 years ago in Boston and married 3 years ago in Washington DC. She is the most fantastic woman in the world and I know she is going to be just an amazing mom. I should be full of joy but I feel really Angry. See, I'm female too. This means that even though we are legally married at both the state and federal level, I will have to adopt this child in order to have a legal right to it. It doesn't matter that I bought the sperm, that I pushed the plunger, that I hold my wife through all her morning sickness, or cook and clean like crazy to rid the house of nausea inducing smells. I will have to pay thousands of dollars, submit to an <u>invasive</u> home-study, and wait months to legally have a right to a child I already <u>love</u> with all my heart. Praying for a day when all families are equal under the law, so all pregnancies can be full of joyous anticipation and not tinged with the anger of injustice.

I slept with a man after our first date.
We stopped talking about a week later due to
differences in what kind of relationship
we're looking for. A few days ago I discovered
I was pregnant with his child. I told him,
and together we decided to terminate the pregnancy.
The situation has caused us to become very close,
very fast... and I think I'm falling in love
with him.

I am sitting here in Washington Square Park delivering my last child at NYU. I sat in this park when I was 16 in the late 60's. I started the first part of my life in this amazing city but have been away since 1978. I have experienced so much since then. I got married had a child who only lived 6½ years and is buried here in New York. I have been through marriages, divorces, birth and death and am a cancer survivor. I cry as I sit here in a place so familiar as I head into ACT 3 of my life which is so unfamiliar. How will I feel when I fly back to California to an empty home.

I will say fly high my child but never forget where you came from.

One of the most important lessons I ~~too~~ learned from working with terminally ill child + especially my little boy who lost his battle with leukemia is "Endings are always beginnings as well"

Tomorrow I will be 56. At this age—
Should one expect birthday wishes of goodwill,
or just need them to believe someone
appreciates your Existance. The son will make
an excuse he had no time or money for a card.
the daughter will send a text. So—what
have I accomplished in these 56 years?
I wish I ~~could~~ knew and I wish their
actions did not define my Existance.

But most of all,
my mom is proud of me,
I know she is.
I love you Mama Bear.
Love, Little Bear.

<u>My story Begins</u> as a child. I have ADHD (No, not the one children are diagnosed with ~~~~ when they behave badly.) As we all know, children are ignorant of such things. So the natural human reaction is to shun what ~~or~~ you dont understand. So making friend was very difficult. It didnt help having a father and mother in the army. I never stayed anywhere longer than 3 years. Making friends was impossible. And kids were so terribly, fucking cruel. So growing up I learned terrible social habits. My mother and my little sister were my <u>ONly</u> friends. When I was ~~8~~ my mother was diagnosed with ~~Brain~~ cancer. The doctors fucked up her first surgery and she couldnt take care of herself anymore. She was still completely intelligent, just couldnt do normal things. When I was 10, my ~~father~~ left. We heard nothing from him besides a check in the mail. So at the young age of 10, I bathed my mother, took all responsibities in the house, and took care of my little sis. They were all I had. On my 13th birthday, my mother died. The 22nd of October. I couldnt even mourn, I had to take care of my sister. A year later, My father wanted us to live with him, so we did, we did not know ~~she~~ he was married again. Or that they just wanted me as a workhorse. I fixed the cars (Im very mechanically inclined) I cleand the house, anything you could think of, I did it. We werent allowed to go out, no phone, no internet, no TV, no vido games, nothing. But I dealt with it until the step mom put her hands on my sister. I snapped. which led to me being kicked out at the age of 17. It was hard. And I havent seen my sister since then. But everythings good now. :) Me and my father are on speaking terms. Im doing well socially, and my lil sis Just turned 18, so shes coming to live with me tomorrow. :) But most of all, my mom is proud of me, I know she is.
I love you Mama Bear.
                        Love, Little Bear.

My Story

Where do I start. I was born in the Bronx to two young parents (mom 20, dad 20). They divorced when I was 5 years old. They used and abused substance and were unable to care for my brother & me. AT 5, my grandmother received custody of us after a long court battle. She (the mother of my dad) raised us the best she could, also being an orphan herself. She was the bread winner, providing all that was needed, but there was one thing she lacked and that was love. She was a wounded soul who could only offer "woundedness". So we, my brother & I got the brunt of that. Her husband was a petifile and was physically abusive (sexually) towards me as a child until about 12 years old, when he passed away. Not able any more to bear the abuse at home I ran away at 17, met my boyfriend and spent a couple of years (5) w/ him. My Mom & dad still addicts lead my younger brother into foster care. I took him out & he came to live w/ me when I was 18. We did the best we could to make ends meet. He at 18 (5 years later) went off to the army and I began a life of healing. At 21 I met Jesus, (Christ) & the love that was lacking in my life was fulfilled. Today I am 30, I seek counseling, and I love my life w/ the assurance that God loves me through His son. my heart has been changed.

I don't know how to start this so I'll just go.
I was 4 years old when I was taken away from my family.
They were addicts and not fit to take care of me. my eight
year old brother was with me. I never was mad at my parents
but at the same time didn't want I life with them. I started
my journey through foster homes and residential programs.
my first house was a disaster, the parents had a daughter
who use to make me sit in the corner till i pissed myself.
afterwards I was sent to a mental phacility due to something the
daughter said I did that I dont remember anymore. after that I was
put in a foster home then moved in with a family to adopt me.
I don't know why but I didn't want it so I miss behaved and to this day
I feel my brother still blames me. all together in my life iwas placed
in 21 different homes in 15 years. I was a troubled angry kid.
In these home I was beaten, abused, and neglected, and so I took
it out on the families that wanted to help. I've made alot of mistakes,
and regret abunch of things, but if I could I wouldn't change a thing
because it made me the nice person I am, and made me appreciate
certain things more. if you are reading this and are deppessed
or have a bunch of regrets, they weren't for nothing.
because life is a journey and every little thing that happens
to you has an impact weather good or bad. look for
tomorrow because that is what you have control over
and above all else, <u>No Regrets</u>. I am no where near
where I want to be in life but I'm happy
to be here

●I am from the great city of Birmingham, AL. Home to The Vulcan, a dead steel industry, and blatant racism that fell through the cracks of the civil rights movement. I have always lived in a very rural area outside of the small city, surrounded by farmland. My family was dirt floor poor. I was the church bus kid. the free lunch kid. The Christmas for kids kid. My father died when I was 15. My mother lost her shit and forgot how to raise a child. My sister got arrested and is now in prison. I raised myself, graduated high school as the first in my family, won over $60,000 in scholarships, and got the hell out of Alabama. I'm 20 years old and completely self-sufficient. I just moved to New York, and I am confident in my ability to guide my own life.

But, I'm still homesick. I still miss the family I don't have. And I still have so much love, and no one to give it to.

I still miss the family I don't have.
And I still have so much love,
and no one to give it to.

My mom is my hero, my best friend, a drunk.
She has always been there for me for everything.
It's hard for me to be there for her tho.

When she is drunk that person isn't my mom.
I know it is a diseas but I can't watch
her crumble. The last time I saw my mom
sober, sane, and normal was when I was 18.
I'm 21 now. It is almost as if the mom I
had to grow up with, my best friend, is no longer
here. I still have hope tho that one
day she will get better and I will have
my mommy back. This may seem childish
but my hope is strong. Sometimes hope
     is   all   we   have.

                HOPE!

Here I am, ... Washington Square Park....,
Feeling somehow down and alone among all
the people in the park.
     I am a Substance Abuse Counselor by
profession and at this time I am facing
a big challenge. I have a 33 year old
son who is abusing alcohol, and only
God knows what else, and I feel that
I am not able to help him.
     That is the paradox of the situation, I
have been able to help many individuals but
I can not help my own blood and flesh.
     Very Frustrating ! ! ! !
Lonely in New York.

I met you years ago through a mutual friend. Several years later we got in contact and you visited me at work. About a year and some change into our relationship, I had to go away to get some help. I had no idea. We had no idea. I haven't spoken to you or seen you in almost 14 months. I've been clean the same amount of time. Whatever the future may be, you will forever be the first person I fell deeply in love with. I'm proud of that. I am proud of our memories and the time and experiences we've shared together. I miss you horribly and I love you beautifully.

I wanted to fucking marry you.

Well now, I'd give anything just to make you some Macaroni and cheese.

My story is one of many alike... I'm a 35 yr. old gay man living in the heart of the concrete jungle, Hells kitchen. I have what all gay men would consider the gay mans dream. A good job, a great Apartment, a partner whom I love dearly & our chihuaha. We have great friends and many good times. However, my partner struggles with pain pill addictions and it is wearing me down. My self worth has diminished and depression has set in. I sleep and hardly eat, worried what may come of my partners out of control addiction. I love him so much & what we have. I know & feel that if he continues this journey of self destruction, the unthinkable will happen. Addiction is Not a fun sickness to deal with. I just hope + pray my love for this great man does not wither away.

Sincerely,

Lost Guy

I came into the hospital drugged up on Haldol and Ativan. I was confused and upset to say the least. I slept through the night like a baby. The next morning was strange. I was there because of a drug overdose the doctors mistook for a suicide attempt. I was sixteen. I remember looking across the room that morning and seeing her. She was a tall girl, talking to another patient. I was immediately embarrassed in my hospital gown. I don't remember exactly how we first spoke. Probably over a card game, one of the only things to do at a psych ward.

She told me she was there over suicidal thoughts, something I knew all too well. We ended up talking a lot, mostly about music. That went on for a few days, until she was discharged. I remember there was no P.C. (personal contact) between patients, but I didn't care. I gave her a huge hug. ~~the~~ That was the last time we spoke for a year.

About a year later, we were on our first date. I had somehow remembered her IM name, and decided to try and talk. We hit it off immediately. I remember how she looked on that first date. Black leather jacket over a black top, fishnet stockings, and bright red lipstick. I remember not paying attention to the movie we decided to see; too busy working up the courage to hold her hand, which I later did. I especially remember my first kiss, at the very end of the movie, as soon as the lights came on.

We dated 9 months, before I had chosen drugs over her. It was one of the worst mistakes I'd made. 2 years passed. 2 years of hours-long late night phone calls. 2 years of "I still love you." 2 years before I had turned my life around, and had the girl I loved back. The same girl I gotten beaten at poker by, and kissed, and learned with. She's sitting next to me as I write this, maybe writing about me. I don't know.

I told my mom I needed to go the the hospital. Little did I know how much going there would change my life. I was depressed and suicidal at the time, and I knew I needed help.

I had been at LIJ Zucker Psychatric hospital for two days when I saw him. He was across the room, still in a hospital robe, so I knew he had just got there. He looked angry. He look like a tough guy that should be on a football team. I was surprized to find out he was as soft as a teddy bear.

We started talking and ended up being best friends in the hospital. We both liked similar music, and I could relate to him like no one else. I taught him how to play poker to pass the time.

When it was time for me to leave the hospital, I made sure to give him my AIM account username, and we promised we would talk. He gave me a big hug even though the nurses told him not to and just said "Fuck it, I'm giving you a hug anyway."

It took him a year to ask ~~me~~ me on our first date, but it was the most memorible day of my life. I remember him being so nervous to hold my hand. And I remember looking up and him kissing me. I knew I loved him that day.

We dated for a while but things got in the way, so we broke up. We never forgot eachother though.

Two years later, we are back together, and more in love than ever. He is the one for me, I know that. We met in a werid place, but I know I was meant to go to the hospital that day, to meet the love of my life.

I WROTE MY FIRST LETTER THIS WEEK AND BOUGHT MY FIRST FLOWERS, I SENT THE LETTER TO YOU AND KEPT THE FLOWERS FOR MYSELF AND I QUIT DRINKING BECAUSE I THOUGHT THAT MIGHT BRING YOU CLOSER TO ME SOMETIME.

ITS DIFFICULT, I'M TIRED OF SODA WATER WITH LEMON AND I LONG FOR INTOXICATION IN ANY SENSE. THE PEOPLE AT AA CLAIM THAT YOU NEVER STOP THINKING ABOUT IT, BUT I WONDER IF I COULD SUBSTITUTE THE NECESSITY WITH SOMETHING ELSE. MAYBE I'LL BE ABLE TO CRAVE SOMETHING LESS LETHAL.

I BINGE ON THINGS, WHETHER ITS MULTIPLE TRIPS TO THE BEACH OR PROFILES ON DATING SITES, I WONDER IF I CAN ONLY CONQUER IF THINGS HAPPEN QUICKLY. I THINK THAT MAYBE I'M NOT THE ONLY ONE.

PS.
PUBLIC SERVICE ANNOUNCEMENT:
CAN EVERYONE WEARING KHAKI SHORTS, BLUE BUTTONDOWNS, AND SUNGLASSES PLEASE AND IMMEDIATELY CHANGE INTO SOMETHING LESS DOUCHEY.

5:45 pm   88°   SUNRIZE 5:25 AM   6/28/12
                  Sunset 8:32 pm.

Been a good work week, Not to hot,
Little Bit breezy.

   Almost 11 months sober, Kid on the
way.

   New ~~city~~ apt with a <u>back yard</u>
in the Fucken city, a BACK YARD.
fucken Amazing.

Been Looking at strollers and they
are alot more expensive then i anticipated.
But thats ok. if it cost every
Cent that i earn, this Kid's going
to have the world.

If i can instill some wisdom Before i
go, it is this;

Try and have compassion for the life
you and all those around you live.

~~Whatever the reason~~

For

~~Whenever~~ Whatever reason, I have a second voice in my head. He doesn't have a name, he doesn't look like anyone specific, and you and I will never see him in real life. He's the figment of my imagination that grew into a permanent fixture inside my brain, and I don't talk about him with other people. (SP)

~~I like to think I'm a well adjusted individual... At least right now. I once took a list of every screwed up moment in my life and shredded them into hundreds pieces, and I like to think that I got over my inner demons. But whenever I have something to wear,~~

I like to think that I'm a well adjusted individual. At some point, I thought ~~about getting myself tested~~ I might be a borderline schizophrenic, ~~or some delusional s~~ but ~~anyway~~ I crossed that off my list after thinking about it. The voice in my head knows that he isn't real. He's also the closest thing I have to a life coach. ~~Growing up~~ Sure, I have my friends and family to go to, but he never judged me when I ~~needed it~~ trust him (which I guess is like trusting myself.) He's always there when I need to think over something, and he has the mannerisms of Danny DeVito. ~~Hez~~ I don't think I would be a well adjusted individual without him.

I often question if I still need the voice in my head. ~~I once talked about him in a college essay, but the college councilor thought I needed~~ He only pops in when I need him, and he hasn't been a detriment to my life. Honestly, you might see me moving my mouth while in deep thought, but that's the extent of it. It's kind of like my brain separates into two parts; my voice is just the rational part of me personified. I hope it stays that way - at least until I get the courage to move on without him.

So my voice do a few things for me:
- life coach
- motivator
- voice of reason
- memory searcher

the life coach and advisor

THE 2nd VOICE IN MY HEAD

Being diagnosed with a mental illness is a little like going to sleep in one location and waking up in an utterly different one. Just when you think you're finally beginning to figure things out, learn who you are, enter the world... It hits. Hard.

Everything you thought you knew about yourself can actually be confined in a single, bulleted list: "Symptoms." It hits so hard that you start to wonder if you're not just one big symptom yourself. The line between "quirk" and "side effect" blur... I've been obsessed with kissing photographs for as long as I can remember, but it stops meaning something when you're constantly told, "Don't." I want to be guilty of original sin because at least no one else thought of it first. I want to be an oscillating function — limitless — but it's hard when I can't help pulling out my eyelashes to make wishes every day.

No one talks about suicide. And people die because of that. So if you see me walking down the street, ask me about my scars.

I don't wear bracelets on my right wrist anymore.
In fact, if I accidentally end up with a hair tie on that
arm, I always move it. There are three scars on that
wrist. Pink and angry and very noticeable if you take
the time to look. I spent four years hiding those
scars. Making up lies about where I was going when I
had doctors appointments. Hiding my medication.
Two suicide attempts later, I ended up in the hospital.
I saw patients get tranquilized. People trying to
escape. A man who asked 18 year old me to be
his baby mama. And it was fun and funny and beautiful
and profound in every way possible. I came face
to face with God. She was waiting for me.
And She held my hand. And it got easier. Slowly
but surely.

No one talks about suicide. And people die
because of that. So if you see me walking down
the street, ask me about my scars.

In a week or so I will float. Now, before I float, the night before, I will check myself In to a mental hospital. Well It isn't a mental hospital any more. The old Belleville hospital is now a homeless shelter. It scares the hell out of me to go there and I really dread The Idea. It is hard because I've been there before. I know how traumatic It was and has taken me nearly 4 years to be able to face it again. I feared for my life constantly, all of life was horrific and unexplainable. People don't expect a person with my education to be homeless. I still cannot fully rationalize it, but in a way, the same way as cancer or other accidents, It has made me far better than I was before. I became massively phobic and recovering has taken years years years years and I'm still recovering from this. floating is part of it. It is a sensory deprivation tank that activates the parasympathtic nervous system. Like sleep but way better.

— Going back to the homeless shelter will tear me apart. —

— floating will put me back together - even better! —

I worked as an RN in Bellevue Psychiatry years ago.

One day, a 20 something year old woman was admitted to my unit for depression. She was catatonic. I went over to her, touched her on her shoulder to let her know I was there, sat down, and talked to her for a couple of minutes (with my very distinctive voice) and then left.

A year later, I was walking with a co-worker through the lobby of the newly opened Bellevue building, and felt the presence of someone walking very closely behind us. Then came a tap on the shoulder. There was a young woman standing there who asked me if I was a nurse. I told her I was. She then asked me if I worked in psych. I told her I did. She then asked me if I was working there about a year ago. I told her I did. She then said → it IS you! I've been hoping to find you one day to thank you for taking out the time to speak with me.

Out of my 30 year career, this was one of my highlights.

You never know when something that you think is not very important can greatly impact another person's life.

When I was 9 years old I asked my mum what bulimia was and she said "it's when models throw up after they eat because they want to be skinny, but still love food. I remember It seemed so logical.

When I was 6 I saw white marks on my mum's hands and she said she's got stiches after she fell off a bike. The lines were straight and parallel on her wrists.

I used to say I would never go clubbing because my dad left the family as he couldn't give up his party life style for me.

When my mother was 16 she ran away from home and shaved her head. I remember thinking not so much "That's crazy, but how ugly.

Now I'm 17 I look in the mirror and I see a short-haired girl, with thights covered in thin white parrallel marks that duffinitely didn't come from falling off a bike.

My hands are contantly shaking because of my malnutrition.

I live 7000 miles away from home and have been for 7 years. I go out nearly every night

Last year my mother was diagnosed with schizophrenia. In a chase to be less like her

I am a lonely teen covered in scars with bulimia, depression addicted to prosac and alcohol.

Don't try to ever not be someone, be you.

102

I STOPPED HERE BECAUSE I JUST WALKED OUT OF A BUILDING ON THE VERGE OF A PANIC ATTACK. MY LEG WON'T STOP SHAKING, BUT I KNOW IT'S GOING TO BE OKAY. I THINK IT JUST HIT ME THAT THE PHRASE "OUT OF MY ELEMENT" ISN'T THE BEST SUITED. I MOVED HERE FROM OVER 800 MILES AWAY, AND I KNOW I CAN CALL THIS PLACE HOME EVENTUALLY. BUT FOR NOW, HOME IS OVER 800 MILES AWAY, OVER 1200 MILES AWAY, AND SOMEWHERE I CAN'T QUITE PUT MY FINGER ON. MY HEART HASN'T QUITE FOLLOWED MY BODY YET, AND INSTEAD IT RESIDES IN CLASSROOMS & BEDROOMS & WITH PEOPLE WHOSE CLOSEST CONTACT IS A CALL AWAY. IT'S HARDER THAN I ANTICIPATED, BUT THIS IS SIMPLY A FRACTION OF MY LIFE UNTIL THE WHOLE. I KNOW THIS WON'T BE A PERIOD OF REGRET, AND I AM FINALLY DONE TELLING MYSELF OF ANYTHING OTHERWISE. I'M FINALLY ON MY PATH OF DISCOVERY, OF HEALING, OF INVENTION, OF GROWTH. THIS IS THE START OF MY STORY.

MY LEG STOPPED SHAKING.

Growing up in NYC wasn't easy as a young abused by my 2 loving parents puerto rican child. From the age of 4 i remember being beaten, whipped, punched until i was 12 and broke my father's back.

At the age of 21 i began a life changing project to hide my scars that i suffered from the abuse. I had an idea and shared it with a friend who was an accomplished tattoo artist. Over the span of 14 years I have successfully covered my scars and body entirely with spiritual tattoos to hide the memories of the 2evil people who raised me.

I'm now a cat lover! I've taken all my life experience and applied it to loving cats and my beautiful girlfriend. It's taken 35 years to forget what my parents did, but i forgave them. Thx mom + dad good job showing me How to be a man. I Live drug + alcohol free and i plan to be married by next year!

I was born in Colombia to a prostitute and a drug addict. I don't know how old I was when I entered the foster care system but I stayed in it until I was 6. Throughout those 6 years I was sexually abused and drugged by my biological father. I was adopted by a beautiful family in the U.S. who I love dearly. I'm beyond blessed and with their help I have achieved far beyond my dreams. Interestingly, what this experience and many others have taught me is that there is no way to move forward without forgiving. Forgive yourself for all your mistakes, they make up a part of who you are; forgive those who harmed you for they too were integral to your growing into who you are. Let the light in. Don't let your past fears hold you back, I refuse to let mine.

What could be more two faced than ~~the~~ the role Greek Life plays in American college culture? I enabled and organized the trafficking of booze to the underage, weed to those who wanted to get high, and the sexual/social lubrication that ~~the~~ results. At the same time I led an organization that raised over a quarter million dollars for cancer research. I would pay bar owners in cash to make their bouncers not ask for IDs, and we'd rent out a whole bar. The next day I would wake up and share eggs benedict with a pastor we were going to ~~open~~ open a soup kitchen with. The more extreme the sins became: buying kegs off a questionable truck, hauling duffel bags of grass on public transit - the more lofty goals we were able to achieve: raising more money, raising more awareness, raising the bar to which Greek Life was held at our University. We won awards for philanthropy and community service, and after the ~~speeches~~ speeches and the thank-yous, everyone would get together and get blackout. The momentum was unstoppable, but I wonder to this day if it was worth it. Did we justify our debauchery by doing good deeds, or were we just addicted to the extreme for better or for worse? Legistlators of America, know this: in raising the drinking age to 21, you have driven the youth of this country away from wine at the dinner table and into the arms of those with corn ethanol and kool-aid mix sitting in smoky rooms. We're waiting for your sons & daughters.

I'm lactose-intolerant ~~but I swear~~ I refuse to give up cheese. The mere hour after my doctor told me about my intolerance I immediately ate a block of cheese and got sick. Totally worth it. I regret nothing cheese 4 ever ♡.

I'll never give it up.

I am recovering from an eating disorder. I thought being thin would ~~always~~ fill all the gaps and give me everything that I wanted. It didn't. I was weak, tired, grumpy and was even more insecure than I was previously. I wondered why nothing was going ~~myself~~ my way. I lost myself. I was a miserable fuck that wanted to evaporate.

2 years into this, I ~~flip~~ finally decided to put myself first. FUCK not eating, FUCK modeling, FUCK what people think. I go out & eat and enjoy my life. I'm not a size 2 anymore, but my life is finally rich. ~~I knew more than I've ever~~

Do not let people control ~~your life~~ your life. DO YOU.

recovery is worth it I promise

YOU everything

Much love, much happiness, with the best intentions,

Stranger

When I look in the mirror, I wonder if what I see is actually what other people see. There is no telling what my appearance means to someone else. All we can rely on is the mirror.

But if you are like me, a dancer, you rely on the mirror a whole lot more to tell you things. Things like, "Is this correct?" And it becomes destructive if you misuse the mirror.

So, please don't let the mirror fool you. Remember that your body is your home. At the end of the day, you live in it, whether you like it or not. And remember, you have no idea what other people see in you, and what they think about what they see. Who knows! Maybe I look like a green alien to you all, but I just don't know it. And who am I to rely on the mirror, then?

I will not disparage my body to anyone, especially not to my girls. I see their bodies as beautiful and perfect, and only by showing that I can love my imperfect body may they also learn to love their own.

I love my body! It is by no means perfect or even desirable by society's standards, but I have decided for myself and for my children that I will embrace love for my body and what it does for me. My arms have gotten stronger since having my two beautiful daughters, because I carry them a lot and I give them all the hugs I possibly can. I love my arms! My knees support my body and allow me to run after my kids. I love my knees! I am not a runner, but my sizeable thighs help me skate very fast (on ice). I love my knees! My belly is all stretched out and flabby from two term pregnancies and one miscarriage, but I love that I grew my sweet babies in my belly and that my belly button still makes my kids laugh. I love my belly! I love my vagina and my clitoris, because I can have amazing sex with my husband or myself!!

I will not disparage my body to anyone, especially not to my girls. I see their bodies as beautiful and perfect, and only by showing that I can love my imperfect body may they also learn to love their own.

I do not disparage other people's bodies either. There are enough people in the world who do that. I will not be one of them.

Hello America,

I'm a black african-american (age 2a)
I'm here (New York) visiting a very good friend whom
I love dearly. I'm from Atlanta. I'm
a dark-skinned female and living in the south
black americans are always concerned about
color. My family, whom are light
complexion always made comments about
my dark skin. My mom (since I was a
little girl) taught me to embrace my color,
my history, and to never let others make me
feel ugly. Not until I went to college
I began to love what I see in the mirror.
Beauty comes from within and in many
colors, sizes, and cultures. To all my
dark skin ladies, embrace your chocolate
skin, it's beautiful and never allow anyone
to make you feel any less. We are beautiful

XOXOXO

L Love my hair. and it's funny that L'm saying because everyone should love their hair because YOU. but for woman of color that self acceptance takes some time.

It'is just now that America is starting to see an "outbreak" of black woman with kinky curls, coils, and fros, because L feel like now is the time for awareness.

L decided to stop preventing the natural grooves of my hair after a break up; now it wasn't because of the breakup that L made this decision, but L felt this would be the right time for a change and honestly L wanted to embrace myself more.

My family didn't "understand me", thought L was negatively changing and thought L needed to see a psychiatrist because L wasn't straightening my hair anymore which was the "right" thing to do. L started to doubt my decision to... go natural... why am L denying my natural state? do I think how I naturally look is not a version of beauty? L decided to ~~take the~~ others unsupportive comments as motivation to show MYSELF.

Natural beauty... beauty is arbitrary and ~~L'm the only~~ if everyone's opinion of beauty differs, why should L try to mold myself to everyone's perception of it?

Embrace yourself. You are beautiful. 9/28/14

I just spent 3 months in an eating disorder facility. I just finished my first 3 weeks of college. I'm slipping back. I'm not doing what I'm supposed to do. I lie about it. BUT I feel good. I am happy, like really haaaappyy. I know what I'm doing but I don't know how long this is going to last. I don't want to go back and I'm SCARED.

114

In high school, my best friend and I used to gush over models with "thigh gap" - that nearly-impossible-to-achieve state of leggyness possessed almost solely by Victoria's Secret Angels whose thighs magically don't touch in the middle. We did this jokingly, splayed out across my bed, flipping through magazines and probably eating chips or brownies. Just silly aspirations. Like dating Chuck from "Gossip Girl." Attending our dream colleges. Thigh gap.

Years later, a recent university grad with a new New York job and budding life. I find suddenly that my thighs no longer kiss past each other when I walk. The first moment I noticed, I shocked myself. I have thigh gap now. Among other gaps: self confidence gap. Romantic gap. That best friend and I no longer speak for reasons I can't understand — perhaps the biggest gap. My life is1 one big mess of ~~gaps~~ gaps and a million hard-to-swallow words (anorexia. fear. failure.) that just can't seem to fill them up.

Dreams are funny, dangerous things. Even the little insignificant ones. Choose them wisely, and cherish them carefully.

When I was 13 years old, I started cutting my wrists. My life felt overwhelming, and making myself bleed gave me something that felt like control. It was a cry for help, yet I never let anyone hear it. I stopped a little over a year later and haven't cut since. I never told a soul until the day of my two year anniversary of being scar free. For some ~~scratched~~ reason, I woke up that morning feeling bold, and I wrote "Two Years ♡" in Sharpie on my wrists. As I wasn't wearing sleeves that day, naturally people inquired about it. It was terrifying telling them the truth, as it was a part of my past not even my best friend knew. Some people were weirded out by it, and most others were visibly uncomfortable. But some friends expressed the same pride I felt at making it this far clean, and they made me promise I would never do it again. My mom was confused as to why I was so proud of myself, but to me it was crystal clear. I had survived two years, and I could survive another two years, and another, and another, and another.

If you are self-harming, please get help. Its not weak to admit you have a problem. It is strong.

2 years, 10 months, 5 days

116

The first time someone saw my ~~cuts~~ in public was on the train. I was on my way to San Francisco to meet a friend (I just moved here from ~~SF~~ California). Two huge black guys walked into the train car I was in blasting music with this whole "we're big and we know it" attitude about them. They turned the music down a little and I heard one of them whisper "hey dude look at her arm." I had a really rough night the night before and my entire left arm which I was holding onto the pole in the train with, was covered in red lines, from above my elbow all the way down to my hand. The second guy looked over but didn't say anything. When ~~the~~ they were getting off, he put his hand over mine and said "hey, stay safe." His friend, who had pointed my arm out in the first place, said "hey dude don't play her, she's too young." But the second the doors closed, the second guy looked back through the small glass window and mouthed "please stay safe," and that's something I'll ever be able to forget. I always wonder what his story is, and I always wish I could say thank you a thousand times more.

When I was 16, I was raped by someone I had to see everyday. I spent years thinking I wasn't special anymore, that I was ruined in some way. I've slept with countless men because I thought that if I didn't give it up, they would take it anyway. I've spent years battling depression and suicidal thoughts.

It wasn't until this past year that I truly started healing. I'm 25 now. It was through a growing relationship with God and the people He has brought into my life that have led me to where I am today. Today I can believe it when I say:

- I am valuable
- I am loveable
- I am not broken
- I am not ruined
- I am worthy
- My body is MINE, no one can take it away from me again.

I hope that if you are reading this and have had similar struggles, that my story brings you some hope that it does get better. Though things may seem dark and empty now, the sun will come and shine again; brighter and warmer than before.

Psalm 30:2 "O Lord my God, I cried to you for help, and you have healed me."

The first time I came to Washington Square Park, I was a camp counselor in college, in charge of ensuring that my high school and middle school-aged charges didn't run off, or buy any weed from the guys murmuring "dime bag... psst... dime bag." (It seems like most of those guys are gone from the park now, but that was the late 1990s.) Within 10 minutes, some strange men dashed up and stole one boy's tennis shoes that he'd taken off to play in the fountain. I started to run after the man, suddenly filled with anger, but couldn't catch him — I was so mad at myself that I had let this happen, as if it were my fault, which was probably more about the fact that I had been raped by one of the other counselors, some water polo player from Villanova, just the week before. I had to go to the hospital for my injuries but declined to report it, and he acted like nothing happened. Then, in the park, he was also watching the kids — I wanted to say something, but I felt paralyzed. It seemed my responsibility to have prevented, like the shoe theft.

I took the kid to Foot Locker and bought him new shoes. It took me more than a decade to realize that you are not what happens to you.

119

September 19th, 2014

    I can't stop lying. I get this incredible rush from watching someone not know that something I am saying isn't true. I'm good at it. Too good. There is something inherently honest in my eyes that no one seems to question. I've obviously been caught before by the people that know me best, but it's like they are almost impressed with how well I tricked them that they can only laugh. But I hate lying. I hate being lied to. So, it's weird to be sitting here and finally writing this down for the whole world to see. I am stopping today. I want people to be honest with me from now on. So I am continuing my life from here on out, honestly. Hope this works.

To my lovely girlfriend,

I know that we just started going out so I suppose that's the main reason for me writing this out rather than telling you. Although I'm ~~young~~ young, I feel old, drained... finished. Before you I was with a girl for 3 years. I loved her and when my father would ask me if she is "The One" I'd smile and say yes. I couldn't have been more wrong. Three years of broken promises, lies, half truths and excuses. So many excuses... but like I said, this note is for you so I suppose I should talk about you. You make me smile and feel wanted. You have no excuses to give. You've kept every promise and have not lied to me. You've breathed new life into me and I no longer feel drained or "old". Simply seeing you makes me smile and every kiss you plant on my lips makes me smile with delight. In a way I'm happy that you dont know my past. You dont know how broken I am. I guess I'm happy because of that because I know that I'm not receiving your affection out of pity. I'm receiving it because you actually care. It's been a while since I've felt cared about. Of course I have a loving family and supportive friends but that wasn't enough. You fill the emptiness that I felt. Getting texts from you makes me happy. Looking at pictures of us lifts my ~~spirit~~ heart. You're beautiful and special to me and I will tell you that everyday for as long as I can. Some might call this puppy love but I have to disagree. I've been a puppy before but now I'm grown. Now I know that what I feel is real. I guess this note was kind of all over the place but it's hard to put what I feel in an order. I wish I had more space to tell you other things but I guess I'll say it to you when the time is right.

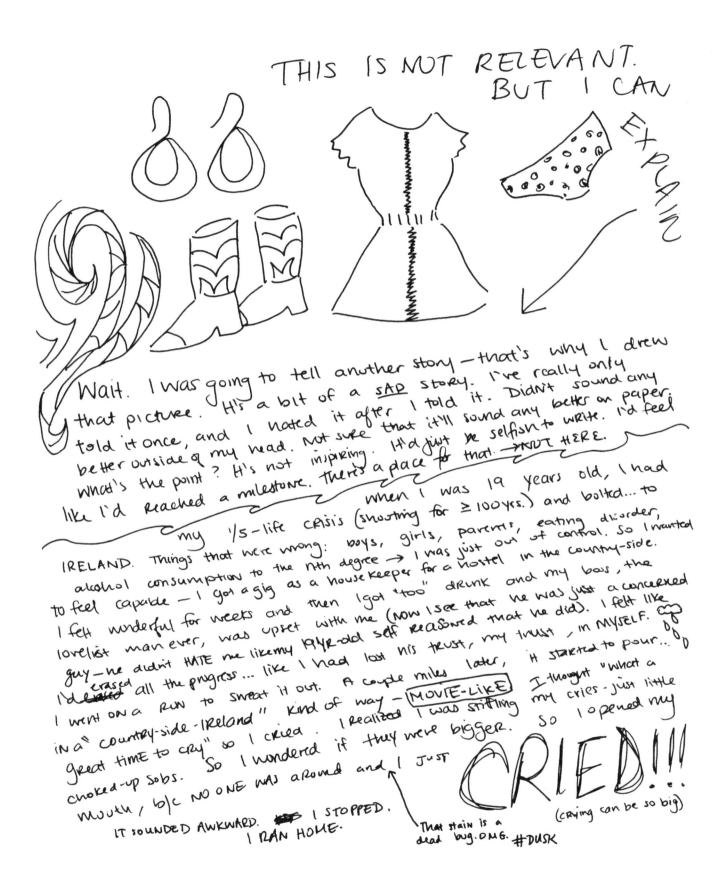

THIS IS NOT RELEVANT.
BUT I CAN
EXPLAIN

Wait. I was going to tell another story — that's why I drew that picture. It's a bit of a SAP story. I've really only told it once, and I hated it after I told it. Didn't sound any better outside of my head. Not sure that it'll sound any better on paper. What's the point? It's not inspiring. It'd just be selfish to write. I'd feel like I'd reached a milestone. There's a place for that. →NOT HERE.

when I was 19 years old, I had my 1/5-life crisis (shooting for ≥ 100 yrs.) and bolted... to IRELAND. Things that were wrong: boys, girls, parents, eating disorder, alcohol consumption to the nth degree → I was just out of control. So I wanted to feel capable — I got a gig as a housekeeper for a hostel in the country-side. I felt wonderful for weeks and then I got "too" drunk and my boss, the loveliest man ever, was upset with me (now I see that he was just a concerned guy — he didn't HATE me like my 19yr-old self reasoned that he did). I felt like I'd erased all the progress... like I had lost his trust, my trust, in MYSELF. I went on a run to sweat it out. A couple miles later, it started to pour... in a "country-side-Ireland" kind of way — MOVIE-LIKE. I thought "what a great time to cry" so I cried. I realized I was stifling my cries-just little choked-up sobs. So I wondered if they were bigger. So I opened my mouth, b/c NO ONE was around and I JUST CRIED!!!...

(crying can be so big)

IT SOUNDED AWKWARD. ~~so~~ I STOPPED.
I RAN HOME.

That stain is a dead bug. OMG. #DUSK

So I opened my mouth,
b/c NO ONE WAS AROUND
and I JUST CRIED!!!...
(crying can be so big)

I got married this year (in March) and almost no one knows. My husband is in the army and is stationed thousands of miles away from me. We are planning on telling my family next year, after I finish my Masters. Every day when I read the news, I worry about him, even though he is stationed in a very safe place. Today is September 11, and once again we are about to begin a long, drawn out engagement in the Middle East. Every time politicians call for stronger military action, I think, is this something that I would sacrifice my husband for? Increasingly, our military is made of people from military families (his father deployed in both Iraq + Afganistan) and for most Americans, these conflicts are abstractions. I think that if everyone had to give a spouse, or a daughter, or a father for the wars, we would never be so militaristic. I just want my little family to be in one place, and safe.

My boyfriend works on planes in the Air Force. I don't know what those planes do or where they go. But I can guess. A lot of the guys he works with ~~or~~ joined up for the same reason he did: to get money to go to school. They don't talk about where the planes are going. They know it's for the service of war, in a vague and abstract way. If they knew the details, would they be upset? Would my boyfriend be proud? I'm proud of all of his hard work and I love him. But I have conflicted feelings about how he's making a living right now. I rarely bring these ideas up with him because I want the limited amount of time we get to spend together to be fun and joyful. And I would never want to force him to come to terms with things that he might not want to at this point. Still, it is not in my nature to feel pride over war.

Sending wishes for peace into the universe.

I'm a first generation East Indian who grew up in California. I studied my ass off, but deferred Ivy league schools to go to West Point, and to serve the country. I write this anonymously because I don't want credit or sympathy. I graduated 18 of 916 from West Point, went to war in Iraq and Afghanistan, ~~can~~ and came back to an ungrateful Indian culture. I'm looked at as the outcast in that society because I'm not the lawyer, doctor or engineer. I struggle to fit in any culture because my identity is a mix of American culture, Indian culture and Military discipline. I've led Soldiers into combat but I can't talk to a girl. I've been shot at and bombed but can't stop jumping at loud noises. I walk around major cities in the U.S. wondering if what I've done with my life is worth it. . . . Then I see children playing in parks and I know its all worth it. I wouldn't change anything. I would do it all over again without changing a single decision. It is worth it.

I was six when he left, six when I thought he forgot about us, six when I thought he ran away. I was too young to understand fully what was going on. All I knew is that my uncle, one of my best friends had left. One day he was there and the next I woke up and he was gone. I didn't understand. I knew that during the week there was considerably less things in his room but I thought he was just getting rid of some of his stuff. I remember running down stairs, running to his room, opening the door... only to find his room completely empty. For the rest of the day I asked my parents, my grandma, and my other uncle what happened; they wouldn't answer me. For months I wondered and prayed that everything was ok. I wondered and worried about him. I was only six when he left and I didn't understand why.

I was only seven when I found out he left to defend our country.

Sometimes I don't understand what my role is in my romanitic relationship. It's very difficult to navigate a love life with someone who was sexually abused. I love my wife to death and I know she loves me, but her trauma is a black cloud that consumes her (and sometimes has it's residual effects on me). I want to fix her and I want her abuser to just fucking die already. Part of me thinks that will make the cloud go away, but I know deep down it never will. I hope I can be her ray of light through this. I could use a ray too, though.

I hope I can be her ray
of light through this.

I am a (fairly) successful young, white, 20-something man from a solidly middle-class suburban family. I live in New York City. I am a college graduate. I have clinical depression.

On October 14th, 2011, I tried to take my life. I was stressed out at school, had few friends, worked long hours, and felt incredibly alone. I walked downtown to jump off the docks at the South Street Seaport (still one of my favorite places—I think it's beautiful), when it occurred to me that I had too many more people to love, and too many things to accomplish. "This is not how the story ends," I told myself.

The next day, I admitted myself to the psychiatric ward of Beth Israel hospital. I spent 4 days there medicated, no contact to the outside world. I was broken. I accepted the fact that a long period of therapy and medication awaited me.

That was 3 years ago. Today, I consider my depression in "remission." I am no longer on anti-depressants and do not attend therapy. I don't need to. I'm finally able to manage my illness. I was one of the lucky ones. It feels like a bad dream.

I still tell my friends I was hit by a cab.

I was feeling depressed today, although as I have improved, I have been able to distinguish less and less why I feel this way. After a lot of searching, I found that it was because I felt that my ideas were not being expressed.

The things that make me the happiest in life are those that allow silent people to express themselves, to allow silent beautys to be found beautiful for the first time.

The park looks brighter as I look up from my page. The people have faces instead of silhouettes.

Thank you.

I'm a 22year old Marine Corps Veteran on the bumpy road to inner peace. I'm trying to make a new life worth living, since I've survived several suicide attempts. In september, I hope to study abroad in Japan and find some stability in my life. Its hard, but I think I can make it. This

summer I'm going to travel and strengthen ties with friends and at the end of it all I hope to be a better person. To anyone reading this, never be afraid of introspect.
At times, being human is inevitably painful, but it can also be amazing. The quote I live by, is:

"Be soft. Do not let the world make you hard. Do not let the world maker you hate. Do not let the ~~world make you~~ bitterness steal your sweetness. Take pride that even though the rest of the world may disagree, you still believe it to be a beautiful place."

When I was a junior in college my favorite
uncle committed suicide. He left my family
only the great memories we shared with him. He has
made me the person I am today. I am writing this
letter after leaving a hospital in the city where
I am a resident. In exactly a year I will be
a doctor and my primary focus of care will be
depression and my goal is to help those who are
in need of someone to help them. No one in my
family knows this and neither does the great
man sitting next to me while I write this. If
you are reading this know that ending your
life is never the answer. It is a permanent
solution to a temporary problem. Life is great
and love could be real if you make it what
you want it to be. Spread happiness and know
that God is Great.

                    —XO

I'm really glad I came across this. I've been experiencing a lot of firsts lately (first role in a film, first time alone overseas) and I'm starting college in the fall. I just feal as if my life is happening right in front of me. It's all incredibly exciting, but scary. I've always wanted to be great, but I'm facing the reality that soon I'll be a real adult and I may very well <u>not</u> be great. Today, though, I remembered a line from (I think) the Hippocratic Oath.

"First, do no harm."

I think that line applies to more than just doctors. In life, we forget that our first job is to do no harm to those around us. Before I can be a great man, I need to be a good person. And at the end of the day, being a good person is enough.

Love,

Anonymous

About seven months ago I was in a very bad accident. I walked out with my head split open, and black and blue marks all over my face. The affects from my concussion are still a constant problem. When I arrived at the hospital the doctor came into the room and said, "I dont know how your not paralized". Those were his first words to me. Not, "thank God your not", but "I dont know how your not". Those words play in my head on repeat every day.

Every time I walk into the dance studio I take a minute to just stare in the mirror. I've never told anyone that I just stare at my reflection thinking that if I had been hit just a few inches to the left, I would not be standing there.

I thank God every day for those extra few inches.

When I was 24 I was in a terrible car accident. My right leg was crushed. Crushed. After several surgeries & several opinions, I was told five words over & over again. "You will never walk again."

It has been eight years since several doctors told me with 100% certainty that I'd never walk again.

I Walk!

It hurts & I still can't run. But I spent the last four hours walking through the beautiful city of NY.

Walking is fantastic. Enjoy it!

Also, don't listen to others if you don't want to believe them. ♡

I am from Canada and I have been a
paramedic for 16yrs. Everyone always asks me
"What's the worst thing you've ever seen?" or
"What's the scariest thing you've ever seen?" and I never really
know how to answer them.
One evening we were called to a potential call for a
"lift assist" which means there are no injuries and a
patient only needs help getting back into bed.
We arrived to find an elderly female lying on the floor
beside her bed. Her husband told us she was fine and
that she just needed help getting back into bed. We assessed
her and found she was NOT fine. She was very close
to death. Her heart was failing and she was barely
breathing. We advised her husband that we needed to
take her to the hospital because she was very sick.
At the hospital, despite futile efforts she died. We
told her husband who asked to see her one last time.
He entered the hospital weeping softly and climbed into
the hospital bed to be beside his wife of over
50 years one last time. He held her....

So when people ask me "What's the worst thing
you've ever seen?" I never tell them.
It's truly int the eye of the beholder!

Ever since I was little, I wanted to be a doctor—I don't know why, but I felt drawn to it & quickly developed a passion for medicine. One summer I attended a medical camp and stayed in a dorm with a roommate. She was beyond smart & had such a natural understanding for medicine; but beyond that she was sweet, compassionate & just wanted to help people—she was the perfect material for a doctor. As the two weeks of camp passed, we got fairly close & once we left camp, we decided to keep in touch. Every few months we would reach out, but we also stayed present in each other's lives through Facebook or Instagram likes. But, this summer, the summer before college & before I would officially be "pre-med", I started to freak out & get nervous about the life path (of being a doctor) that I chose. Not soon after I started to doubt myself, I got a text from a mutual friend saying that my friend, my roommate from med camp had died. Heart attack. At 17. Perfectly healthy. I was utterly distraught. But in that moment, I knew what I had to do: I had to push my worries aside & trust my passion. I had to work hard, as hard as I possibly can to become the best doctor I could ever become, because she'll never get the opportunity to do so. I'm going to do it for her & for all the people like her: the ones with dreams & aspirations that will not get the chance to chase them.

—The Aspiring Trauma Surgeon

THE SECRET TO HAPPINESS
IS LOVE + SELF LOVE.

THE DAY THAT CHANGED MY LIFE WAS ON A SUNDAY, ABOUT NOON + I WAS HUNGRY. I GET DRESSED AND GOT IN THE CAR; EMPANADAS WERE ON THE BRAIN SO OFF I WENT. I STARTED BACK TOWARDS MY HOUSE AND FOUND MYSELF AT A CROSSROADS. AS I MOVED FORWARD, ALMOST INSTANTLY AN ON COMING VEHICLE HIT MY DRIVER'S SIDE. I CAN STILL FEEL THE IMPACT. I LOST AND REGAINED CONSCIOUSNESS WITHIN 2 MIN OF IMPACT. CAME TO WITHOUT A SCRATCH ON MY BODY. MY THOUGHTS + CHARACTER WERE FOREVER ALTERED. I QUESTIONED LIFE + MY PURPOSE, FINDING INNER PEACE AND ONENESS. THE SECRET TO HAPPINESS IS LOVE + SELF LOVE.

At age 62 I was at loose ends with my life. I had made tofu & miso in the 70's, raised 4 kids and farmed organically in the 80's and had a small masonry business. In the 90's I returned to our family farm when my father retired and farmed 800 acres. My kids who were now on their own and my wife left. I travelled sold my equipment, leased the farm and moved to San Frasisco and then farther up where I worked for a non-profit seed company.

After another relationship didn't work out I decided to do something I had wanted for years, join the Peace Corps. I was accepted and sent to Malawi, the 5th poorest country in the world at the time. But To reach my village I had to ride a mini-bus for 1½ hours - a risky business in itself, and then ride a mountain bike 2½ hours over hills, through rivers and around potholes big enough to swallow a car.

It was an interesting experience as well as disillusioning. The people in my area made about one dollar per YEAR! They thought America contained only rich white people with no problems. They wanted a better life but due to their colonial past, corruption, poverty, poor education and lack of resources there was not much hope.

I wish that humanity can become aware that we are all connected - to each other and the universe and realize the earth has enough for everyone to have what they need and be happy.

I've loved Japan for as long as I could remember. When I was a kid, I had this Japanese teacher ~~who~~ who exposed a whole new world to me that was so much more than my small corner in Brooklyn. ~~There~~ As time went on, ~~my~~ it came to my attention that everything I liked as a kid came from Japan. My toys, the video games, my CD player, power rangers, bullet trains, everything. I was in ~~LOVE~~.

8 years later, I had an opportunity in High School to stay with a host family for a month. I applied, but looking back on it, I was scared and really dropped the ball on going. I wasn't ready to leave the nest.

In college, I got annother opportunity to study abroad for 4 months. I applied, got accepted for the spring semester, and left school determined to follow my dreams. I poured my life savings into it and although I was scared to go, I ~~knew~~ knew this would change my life forever.

1 week before my flight, the tsunami hit Japan. Because of the nuclear power plant disaster, the government banned U.S. citizens to travel. I lost most of my money through various reimbursement loop holes. I was left back a semester because it was too late to go back to school. And I cursed the world.

I failed to realize that I was alive and well at home. God looked out for me and just decided that I wasn't ready yet. I feel lucky everyday now for that small blessing.

I poured a lot of sweat, blood, and tears into it, but I'm leaving for Japan next month. It's only for a week, and it's just me doing it alone, but I'm ready this time. I'll be backpacking through Kyoto, Osaka and Tokyo. I've been enrolled in Japanese classes for the past 9 months too, so I've got that going for me. When I come back, I will apply to teach there too.

Moral of the story. Don't give up. Follow your D..R...E..A...M...S

"I'm grateful for racing analogies," he said, "because I think they help make sense of life."

And sometimes I think I can relate to that too because I know what it feels like to run and run ~~with my~~ lungs sucking in air before my body is ready for more.

I think I hit the ground running when I moved to New York after I graduated. I think about feet a lot these days. The first book I ever read by myself was called the Foot Book. "How many many feet you meet."

Some one was talking about a thing called Dunbar's Number once. It's a special number of people you can hold in your head and remember before the ones on the edges start falling out. I thought that was really unfair that we can't care about all of the people always. But maybe if everyone cared enough about their Dunbar's Number-worth, ~~no~~ wherever they happen to be, then everyone in the world would be covered and everyone would be taken care of.

But that isn't the case.

And I know because I work at a homeless shelter for 18-20-year-olds. We ask the residents a bunch of questions when they first come so we can know how to help best. One of the questions is "How many people inside your family would you say have been supportive to you?" And another is, "How many people outside your family have been supportive?" More often than not, I record a double zero. And I think, what would life be like if zero people loved me?

My job is not easy and it would be easy to lose hope. But I do not lose hope because I know every person has the power to change zeros into ones. Running races aren't easy either, and I will run in that hope. I will run this life-race with perseverance; being loved myself beyond measure, I will do my best to love all the feet I meet.

This morning my boyfriend & I had brunch outside (it was not good). A homeless man walked up & started digging through a trash can, pulling out coffee cups and combining them into one clear Starbucks cup. Right after he left a man walked up & looked in the trash. My first impression was that he was an average man going to the park to read the paper. Upon closer inspection I noticed that the button down shirt he was wearing was torn in several places, his shoes were worn out. It seems he was homeless too but it just seemed so much sadder than the previous guy. He looked like ~~one~~ one of my friend's dad. I've thought about him all day.

I also saw a woman wearing a helmet. I fought the urge to tell her that she should wait until she gets to her bike before putting it on.

7/21/14

At the current moment, I am "homeless" as well as "unemployed." But things seem to be better now than back when I was living in a house. I chose to be unemployed temporarily so I can travel to see all 50 states. I'm from Texas, but am writing this in New York. I live in my car, shower at Planet Fitness gyms all over the country. I'm filming and documenting my journey as I go and upload my stories online for all to see that ANYBODY can pursue a dream or goal. For money, I've built a musical instrument out of PVC pipe that straps to my back. I perform this instrument in the street. As it turns out, I make more with this instrument hourly than any job I've ever had. At the end of this journey, I will have a resume of my talents recorded and I will have put myself out there.

I am 19. I am Homeless, but I dress well enough the strong isn't Attached. But there is still A feel of failure. I would be Alone if it weren't for my Beautiful girl and our PUPPY. I've never Been more happy to have nothing. This is not what I Planned, But It's what I needed.

When I was 16, my father was diagnosed with terminal brain cancer. The disease ate away his mind and body, paralyzing and blinding him. The man that had been the tall and mighty tree of my childhood withered away into a fragile old man - not even the shadow of who I'd remembered him to be. A month after graduating high school, my father passed away at home at 7pm on July 7th. Dying in the real world is nothing like the glamorous demise of a leading man in a Hollywood movie. They never depict the violent last gasp, the slack-jawed look of a dead man's empty gaze, or the yellow pigment the skin takes on once the heart stops. The mighty tree, present in all of my happiest memories, was a corpse in my home. The undertaker came that night, zipping my father up into a black parcel ⋯~~~~ taking my Daddy away.

My partner might be homeless in a few months
I am going to stay with her no matter what, but I am
worried about what my friends and family will say.
It's not her fault.   And I can't just stop being in love.

I woke up one morning but something felt different. I was on a ~~beach~~ beach. I don't know how I got onto this beach or what beach but there was profanity drawn with a sharpie on my arm. Last night was a complete blur. I met someone special. All I remembered about him was that he was the most wonderful person I've ever met. And now I had know idea where he was, or what his ~~first~~ name was. All I had left was a very inappropriate drawing on my right arm. Where was he? Where had I last seen him? These were questions rolling through my brain. I had no idea where to find him. ~~~~

I slowly got up. My head felt like a ball of lead and my shoes were missing. I got up on two feet and stumbled for a second. A child playing in the sand was staring at me. What should I do? I had no possibilities. ~~because~~

I WAS HUNG OVER AT THE DOMESTIC AIRPORT I USED
TO WORK AT, IN A SMALL CITY SOMEWHERE IN EUROPE.

JUST TO BE CLEAR, I WAS WORKING AT THE TIME.
MY BOSS TOLD ME TO GET UP, THERE WAS
SOMETHING I HAD TO SEE. I RELUCTANTLY
AGREED AND ASKED WHAT IT WAS, WHILE I
MADE AN EFFORT TO MAKE IT SEEM LIKE
STANDING UP WAS THE HARDEST THING EVER
SO THAT IN A WAY I ALREADY "WORKED"
THAT DAY. HE BRINGS ME TO THE
CHECK IN COUNTER AND POINTS OUT THE
CUTEST LITTLE THING (NOT IN A "THROW ME IN
JAIL AND KEEP ME AWAY ↑ girl FROM ELEMENTARY SCHOOLS"
KIND OF WAY).

THAT DAY I MET MY WIFE. SHE WAS
THE CUTEST LITTLE THING THEN AND STILL
IS 4 YEARS INTO OUR MARRIAGE.

OH, AND I HAVEN'T LIVED IN THAT PLACE SINCE,
CAUSE I CHASED HER TO NYC 3MONTHS LATER

AND NEVER LOOKED BACK

I've always believed in finding love in unexpected places. One day, taking the subway home after a doctor's appointment and fighting a massive infection, all I wanted to do was crawl in bed and rest. The young guy sitting next to me started making small talk and asked me how to get to Columbus Circle. He then asked me where I was heading and if he could take me out for dinner. Surprised he found my red eyes and runny nose attractive, I declined but he asked if he could e-mail me. I obliged, and he held my hand an extra long moment as we parted. The next day, I get an e-mail from him with the worst-written erotic "story" I'd ever seen. He ended the e-mail by asking if I would like him to do those things to me. I haven't ruled out meeting Prince Charming, but I doubt it's going to happen on the subway.

Things said before first kisses: 👁

1. "I don't know what I'm doing." "It's not rocket science"

2. "Can I kiss you?" "... Sure."

3. "I think you brought me here to kiss me." "No, it's just a pretty view ... but I did want to kiss you." "I'm always right."

4. "Oh my god, stop talking." "Why did you have to - "

5. "Wait."

Today in my acting class a girl said that her worst fear is that she is incapable of loving. And then I thought — I have kissed 9 boys and I have never been in love. I've had nine open hearts and warm hugs and long looks and awkward fumbling and still I feel nothing for these boys. In my head they are just stories to tell, not even people who lead perpetual lives.

I feel scared.

Age: 18

Number of people I've kissed: 43
Number of people I've kissed on a dare: 25

Number of boyfriends I've had: 4
Number of girlfriends: 1

Number of people I've slept with: 17
Number of boys: 16
Number of girls: 1
Number of threesomes: 1

Number of sexual partners
                who've made me orgasm: 1

Number I've faked it for: 0
Number who've noticed I didn't finish: 1

Reason why I didn't finish: I didn't love them

Will I ever tell you that: maybe

Will I ever love you: I'll tell you the same thing
                I say when we're having sex
    "I'm really close"

Being one of the only out gay girls at an all girls' Catholic high school was ~~different~~ probably the most difficult thing I will ever have to deal with in my life. Rumors, gossip, bullying, all that good stuff. It was pure torture. When I was nominated for prom queen as one of 5 in my class, I knew I would not share that experience with anyone other than my girlfriend. After fights with the administration and saying I wouldn't take the title unless she was my escort, I was the first person at my high school to walk with a girl at prom. That moment gave me the strength I have today; the strength to travel, the strength to pursue music, the strength to be open about who I love, and the strength to be honest with myself. From the absolute darkest of points to now, I wouldn't have changed one step I've taken to get here.

The day after home coming I took a bra from your room. Even though that was years ago, I'm wearing it now. How many people can say they've got a bra that belonged to their ex-boyfriend?

You taught me so much about gender and love and I'm so glad I met you. Good luck transitioning to become the man you truly are (so the world can see). They say you'll never make it in politics because you're trans... I know you'll prove them wrong.

P.S. I'm sorry about the terrible things I said when you broke my heart. I didn't mean any of it.

P.P.S. I wish I had the courage to tell you that I'm asexual But every time I tried, you pushed me away.

I broke up with my girlfriend from 5 years eight months ago. It was terrible. All I wanted to do was cry and eat blueberry and lemon cookies. Before this trip I realized I didn't want to lose her or forget her. Ever. I realized I want her back.

When I return to Colombia I'm gonna ask her to marry me. Gay marriage isn't legal down there but I don't care. All I want is to spend my ~~days~~ mornings next to her. I don't know why but I love the way she smells in the morning. Is ~~saw~~ a sweet smell that feels like home. I already bought a ring. I hope she says yes.

I'm here, at Washington Square Park, sitting next to someone who I can see me spending the rest of my life with. Unfortunately, he is a man and I am a man, so it's somewhat complicated. Not because we are not compatible or because we don't love each other — because we do... However, his religion is standing in the way of us being together. He was taught that same-sex relationships is against God's laws, which makes NO sense because I thought God was the creator of ALL, including us — including our love. I'm just sayin'... Either way, I understand his challenge (not God's, but the man I love) AND I can be empathetic towards him. In the end, though, I think it WILL work out the way that it's meant to AND I don't mind waiting until he figures it out. Because I did. It took some time, but I did... And I really don't know what else to say. I'm just dedicating this entry to him and I. Maybe one day, I will see this printed somewhere and I can read it at our wedding... I know, right. I have faith in God's intentions, even if they don't always seem to make sense. Meanwhile, I'm atheist. Can you imagine? But I love him anyway.
Thank you!

The first time I fell in love, I was 20.
He became my best friend but not my boyfriend.
He already had someone back home.
He was an exchange student from Tennessee,
6ft1 basketball playing buttondown wearing southern
gentleman. The first time we met, we had a
snowball fight.

I don't remember anything about him now. The
night before he left for Tennessee we had a
bonfire with our friends. I told him he made
me a better person, he said I made him
a happier one. When he left the next day
I gave him a hug and he smelt of mouthwash.

There's this lost boy I keep finding at different times in my life. First, when ~~when~~ we were nine — me, being chased and terrified. Him, defending me by pushing the other boy into the mud. It's a moment I remember so clearly — looking back frantically, expecting my aggressor. Instead, I saw him and my child's mind was able to recognize, even then, the warmth in his eyes.

Again, when we were twelve and thirteen. I harbored a strange aversion to him for a reason I didn't know. My mother always had this secret smile on her face whenever I brought him up. I remember a sunset reflected in lake water, a rope dangling above the shallows and the strength of his arms when he pulled me in for ~~aa~~ an unexpected hug.

Last, when we were eighteen. We'd changed. I had a sense of direction by then. The perfectly planned, expected trajectory. He had nothing. I sensed the ~~been~~ sadness in him and found it beautiful. I wanted to stay in the backseat of that car, in his hands, with his mouth. I almost did.

But I broke everything, like I always do.

So, here it is, my message to him:

Come find me. Come find me. This time, I will stay.

THIS IS ALL I WANT - JUST KISS ME WITH YOUR EYES AND PROMISE YOU WILL NEVER DRIFT AWAY --

YOU HAVE YOUR LIFE AS I HAVE MINE - AND I KNOW I CAN NEVER ASK FOR MORE - SO SOMEHOW WE KEEP HOLDING ON...YOU HAVE YOUR LIFE AS TIME GOES BY - AND SOMEHOW WE STAY CONNECTED...THAT SOMEHOW SOMEHOW KEEPS GROWING STRONGER - THAT IS A LIE FOR I FEEL SO MUCH MORE - THERE IS A BURNING DEEP INSIDE...I STILL FEEL THE SAME...KISS WITH OUR EYES - AFTER 20 YEARS - LIKE BEFORE WE WILL HUG AND - NO - KISS WITH OUR EYES - AND...NO - KISS WITH OUR EYES - IN JUST A FEW MORE DAYS - I KNOW YOU ARE COMING TO NEW YORK

My First Date

She told me that the movie was 'five to seven'. Cool, I thought. Starts at five, ends at seven. My Father dropped me off at the theater at 4:45. Nervous and excited, I sat on a bench in the lobby and waited. Five o'clock rolled around and the thought that I was being stood up on my first date started entering my head. This thought grew stronger and stronger, until it was 5:20, at which point I found a phone and called my dad to pick me up from the theater. Feeling lonely and rejected, I slumped into the passengers seat. My dad insisted that I call her house to find out what happened. She answered, and I sheepishly asked her what the deal was. "What do you mean?" She asked, "We're seeing the movie at 6:55. Five minutes to seven. 6:55."

I met up with her at the theater soon afterward. We saw the movie and everything went according to plan.

It was our first and last date.

There is this girl. We met two years ago and since then, time has been amazing. Not easy, of course, different countries, different continents even. We finally managed to move to New York together and I know the wait was totally worth it. We are not married yet, but I know we will. We don't have kids yet, but I know we will. It is a strange feeling, but if you know, you know. I know. I know I will be with her forever and it is a great feeling I wish everyboby will experiences one day. And since yesterday I know one more thing. We knew that our first kid, if it is a girl, will be named Emma. It made my day today and it excites me to know my kids name. It's like that. If you know, you know. I hope you know what I'm talking about.

I'm meeting the boy I will marry half-way from where he lives and where I live. We made this decision, our "New York City" decision, two years ago in a ~~bar~~ bar of Hamburg's red-light district. We were both in love with the idea, but the idea seems not to be in-love with us. It's incredibly frustrating how many complications come with starting a life in a new country when two different passports are involved. We don't know where we will live, who we will work for, how long it will take for our hopes to vanish or our bank accounts to be emptied, but I am absolutely sure we will find a place where we can both be happy and able to live legally. And eventually, in that place we will have a daughter named Emma. She will have dark hair, light eyes, and an inherited tenacity that will allow her to do anything and go anywhere. I love her already.

If homeless people hit on you and you reject them, don't feel that bad because they probably do that to everyone.
Also, it's probably my dad.

When I was 15, my math tutor stole me away from my boyfriend, who was also 15. My math tutor was 35 and it was this whole big, intense mess. Don't get involved with men who are that old when you're only 15, because if they genuinely believe that it's ok to do that, then ... they are out of their mind.
But if you wanna learn a lot about life really fast, then go for it.
That was deep.

It was only two days before I had to fly back to New York. The whole summer I lived for the moments where the boy from across the office would say hello to me, and for the first time we found ourselves outside of the office walls, together. Just the two of us. We drank tea and then walked what felt like the length of the whole city. Talking about our hopes, our deepest fears, our lives, if my feet would have let me I would have walked all night with him. Of course, feet only last so long, so we found a relatively quiet place to sit. As more time passed, suddenly it stopped. Time came to a halt when he looked at me with the most beautiful eyes I have ever seen, and he said quietly, "So, by now you've probably guessed, I'm attracted to you."

I spent every possible minute I could in his arms. He sang for me, he played his guitar. Time took the most exquisite breath, and then it exhaled and I was on my 7:00am flight, 3,000 miles away.

I remember when we said goodbye I almost said I loved him. And, you know, I do love him. We were only given two days, and now we are separated by many miles, but I have faith that the universe will bring us back together once again.

I really want to sleep with my therapist. He is tall and dashing with these penetrating blue eyes. I've been seeing him in sessions for over a year. He kept me from killing myself. I think part of his help is what attracts me to him. He makes me feel safe and okay. And he's hot. Sometimes after speaking about something we'll go silent and just look each other in the eyes for about 5 seconds. Then, he closes his eyes, seeming to fight against his urges, and then we carry onto the next topic. Well today, I told him I was attracted to him for the first time. We agreed to talk it all out next week, or whenever I feel I want to. I'm excited to tell him how I feel, and what I'd like to do to him and with him, all while he sits across the room, listening. That will be satisfying enough. No physical contact necessary.

As I write this, I'm sitting next to my 'boyfriend.' I put that in quotes 'cause he's only my boyfriend to the public; in private, he's "Daddy". I never thought I'd be a part of this lifestyle. I'm 21, he's 39. Almost no one in my life knows about him. They wouldn't approve. Some people think our lifestyle involves "sexualizing things meant for children". Some people assume I'm some kind of 'gold digger' or have 'daddy issues'. (I love my "bio-daddy" very much.) Some people don't understand what we could possibly have in common to begin with. But here's what I know:

• he's the most understanding person I know. We understand and relate to each other better than anyone else in my life.

• he's been there for me when no one else has been willing or able to. He makes time no one else does for me and makes an effort no one else does.

• I feel more comfortable with him than anyone else. I can wear flats instead of heels and read "the Gruffalo" instead of the Times. There's no intentional "sexualizing of anything", but an understanding that a lot of 'adulthood' and 'maturity' is like, arbitrary anyway.

• I feel like more of a 'woman' than I ever have. I've never been more in-tune or in love with my sexuality or my femininity — no one's ever appreciated it like this.

• my grades have improved. My self-esteem has improved. I get more sleep + I've lost weight.

living this weird double life thing is worth it. I love my "Daddy" more than anything in the world.

Hi people,

I love my wife, let me tell you about her she is columbian, i'm American — we met through a Friend and as soon as I met her I knew she was the one — why?

let me tell you — she is smart strong pretty + sexy.

we've been together for 18 years — and have a 15 year old Daughter.

I met her after I got out of a Relationship with a stripper that was on going for 3 years. She was 19 and I was 33.

the story is I was loaded when I met the stripper, and I spent loads of cash on the stripper. What fun we had + Great sex!

I bought her a set of "Breast implants", paid her rent, gave her cash — and after 3 years she splits with me for a guy named ~~____~~ who the fuck is ~~____~~?

well my friends I was devistated, and very sad. But after 6 months I started to meet other women, then met my wife.

She Blew me away — No money ever came up and we had a lot in common.

I am still with her — and some times think about the stripper, But I am happier without her.

My wife makes all the Difference in the world to me.

I will never leave her.

Oh — by the way stay away from strippers!

Bronx Boy

Hi!

My name is Stranger and I... am a recovering pornography addict. Even now, anonymously, I hesitate to say it. My problem started when I was 15 years old. I'm now 26. I'm not perfect, but I've come a long way. The hardest thing was talking about it to anyone. It took me two years to do that. For three years I was able to clean up my act as I prepared for and then served a mission for my church. I've experienced a lot of shame, but I've worked through it and have learned how to love myself in spite of my shortcomings.

You might be snickering - this kind of addiction is often treated as a joke in society, but it's real. It has caused a lot of heartache in my life. The greatest thing is that I've had the people I care about stay by my side through the darkest of times.

I'm now dating a beautiful girl who gets it and is patient with me. Human beings can be pretty amazing creatures when you open yourself up.

It's a beautiful evening in Washington Square Park. People are here with their friends and lovers. Buskers are busking. Birds are singing. What a gift to be alive.

September 5, 2014   (Female, 27)

I moved to New York last year to do something with my life.
I've always wanted to be an artist/writer/designer/ all around creative
polymath. I'm starting to have some success. Just got a piece into Cleis Press!
Also, I'm better than most of the people in my fashion program. Not to be
a jerk. But I am. It's objective.

I've struggled with Asperger's Syndrome for my whole life. It was
hard growing up, but I sort of found my niche in college because a lot of
the students there had issues like me. I made friends with a lot of socially
awkward people, bipolar people, and people who were brilliant but couldn't
really do much about it because they had broken homes in West Virginia.
I didn't have to look for these people. We found each other.

I came to design school because I did really well managing an
upscale consignment shop back home. But I bombed my internship.
I'm lonely. I joined a support group for other people with AS. I met
a guy there. We were together for 6 months. He did everything I told
him to do. Even kinky sex. I wore the strap-on. He took it. I don't think
I'm going to find anybody this easy to be with again, but I didn't love
him.

Now I'm looking for friends at a BDSM club (lots of socially awkward
people at those). A writer's group. Random bars. I'm dying to get loaded +
tell someone my story. There's a lot. I could go on forever. But it's really,
really hard to have anything organically happen like that in this city.
Everybody's working hard. Everybody's sizing each other up, only wanting to
allocate their free time to whoever they think can get them somewhere.

I'm dying to hear some stories that will humanize this place. But so far,
it's tough finding anyone who has the time to tell me.

After 9/11 I lost my job. I had a son who was a toddler at the time and without a job I couldn't support him. I went ~~on~~ on over 50 interviews and was having no luck because so many people were out of work. I'd be 'overqualified' for some, or just not have the right credentials. I was starting to fall behind in rent.

Having no prior knowledge of the 'sex industry', I ~~knew~~ started an escort agency where the women were treated fairly and got a larger percentage (by far) than the 'average' agency, so I built one of the most lucrative ~~most~~ agencies in the city in a few months. I only kept enough money each month to pay my rent and take care of my son. During this time I still was interviewing for 'real' jobs in the day-time, and then handling the business I'd created in the evenings.

I had a lot of moral conflict as a woman and as a mother, running this sort of business. I made it a point to meet ever girl (women) that came to work for me and got to know them on a personal level. The women who worked for me often told me that ~~they~~ they managed the work as if they were a coin with two sides, and neither ever met. They had learned to compartmentalize. Most of the women had children, most other's in their lives, like in ~~mine~~ mine, had no idea of this '2nd life'. In this, we all bonded.

As soon as I got a 'real' job, I disbanded my creation and kept in touch with a few of the women as friends for a few years. It was in ways such a relief to leave that 'world' behind, and I knew my women would not get the respect nor money they'd made when we worked together, but the risk, the life, the sheer amount of work making sure all of my girls were safe, respected and not being forced by someone else to work was exhausting. I loved the women who worked for me. It, however, completely changed my view of men.

I could not care a less about being
remembered in a public way.
It is enough to have been loved.

I don't know what my earliest memory is really. Those sort of things concertina in over the years. I do remember my brother finding a mice nest then throwing the baby mice into a fire. I couldn't at that time be conscious of the pain they felt but I was fascinated and scared. Though I lived in a fairly hard world I don't think that I liked the violence of it. Strange because I ended up in the Vietnam war.

The happiest time of my life is when I wake up spooned with my wife. After 28 years I get happier every day with my being with her. The first night we met she had me taste some chocolate pudding off her finger then we fucked and fucked and fucked and then we fell in love.

The first thing that I noticed about her was ~~her~~ that she was kind. She is also loyal and courageous. We continue to get to know each other even after 28 years and there is a deep deep love & trust & joy between us. She has been the kindest person in my life or at least the one that I have most recognized and allowed.

I could not care a less about being remembered in a public way. It is enough to have been loved.

There are so many things that my family, friends & so on don't know about me. I suspect that is true of everybody. But then they probably know things about me that I don't know.

I am a 21 year old girl who lives in manhattan. My best friend would have to be my mother. I love her with all of my heart. I sometimes feel I depend on her too much but whatever. Now when it comes to my father I am not so sure about him. My mother and father have been divorced since I was in the 5th grade. I am not close to my father at all especially now since he moved to Jersey and has a new family. I love my dad of course but have zero respect for him. I don't tell many people why my mom & dad got divorced but in my mind I blame it on Sept 11, 2001. This might sound stupid but I don't care. See my stepmom her previous husband died on 9/11. He was a NY firefighter. My dad is also a firefighter as well. During the whole 9/11 madness firefighters were sent to different families who have had lost someone on 9/11. Well that is how my father met my current step mom. My father cheated on my mother with this other woman. If 9/11 never happened my parents would still be together. I would bet $$ on that. ~~~~~~~~~~ ~~~~~~~~~~ -TODAY TODAY??
I want to be ok if i never spoke to my dad again.

176

I cheated on you so many times that I lost count. I could say that I couldn't help myself, but the truth is I could have. There was always a choice. The choice to talk to her, the choice to buy her a drink, the choice to feel her body with my hands, the choice to kiss her, the choice to drag my tongue upon her lips and into her mouth, the choice to follow her home, to walk up her stairs, to pin her up against her door, the choice to undress her, to fuck her, to leave, to come back home to you, the choice to crawl back into our bed with you, the choice to tell you nothing, and the choice to keep doing it again and again and again.

I was miserable. I kept hoping you'd catch me. We could have fought, had a big blow out, friends taking sides, the whole kabuki fucking theater of violent separation. Instead I said it wouldn't work one night over dinner, casually, like saying I didn't feel like dessert or another drink. I looked you in the eye and told you that I didn't love you, which was a lie. I said things about independence, accountability, freedom, living lives, bullshit words my father said once, maybe even a line or two from a film. But the truth is I just didn't want to be miserable anymore. I didn't want to make you miserable. I hope you're not. I'm slowly unwinding the knot of misery that sits in my breast like a frozen river.

I just found out you're seeing someone new. I hope he adores you. I hope he's kinder to you than I was. I hope that that man can return all that love you have to give, as I could not. In cheating you, I cheated myself.

My current boyfriend told me he loved me after only a month of dating. It took me a little longer to say it back, but not that much longer. To be honest though, I don't think I really meant it til months later. It was stupid, really. We were lying in bed playing each other terrible music from our childhoods, and all of a sudden "Super Bass" by Nicki Minaj came on. I know literally every word to that song, and in my white middle-class way I own it so naturally, I rapped the whole thing. When I finished, he just got this look on his face like I was the most beautiful person he'd ever seen. I figured that anyone who could love that side of me in that way was right for me. Now when I say I love him, I mean it with all my heart.

July 21st, 2014

I MET A GUY. A NICE ONE. ON TINDER.
WE WENT ON A BUNCH OF DATES, THEN HE
STARTED BEING DISTANT WITH TEXTING.
THEN I DECIDED I WAS DONE WITH
HIM BECAUSE HE WAS BEING DUMB.
HE APPOLOGIZED AND SENT ME EMOJI
FLOWERS TWO DAYS AGO, BUT HASN'T
SEND A WORD SINCE. I'M NOT SURE
IF I SHOULD SNAPCHAT HIM OR SOMETHING.

NONE OF THIS MATTERS BECAUSE I'M
GOING OFF TO COLLEGE SOON; & THEN WE
WILL PROBABLY NEVER SEE EACH OTHER
AGAIN. IT'S A SHAME BECAUSE HE IS REALLY
AFFECTIONATE AND HAS A GOOD COCK,
WHICH IS IMPORTANT TO ME.
I'LL BE FINE THOUGH

I guess you can say my story is about image and perspective. As a young teenage girl, my image to others is the girl who is a nerd, gets good grades in school, plays sports, writes for the newspaper and the like. One day, something inside of me snapped, and I wanted to do something crazy. Naturally, being a high school student, that included sex and drugs, (and of course the sex was with my drug dealer). I'm not really sure why I wrote about this, I guess it's just to talk about the things I regret. Every braniac has a wild side. That's cliche....

6/29/12

I hate clichés. I hate them, I hate them, I hate them. When we peer-edited essays in high school, I was always the picky bitch who would strike out entire lines, draw giant Xs, leave harsh comments in red pen. "CLICHÉ." "BE MORE ORIGINAL." "THIS IS SO TIRED + BORING."

One of my least favorite expressions was about feeling the floor dropping away from under one's feet. Such crap, I thought. Shock is such a big feeling; surely there are better ways to put it.

Turns out I was wrong.

Because when you called last week, that's exactly what I thought of, exactly what I felt. Why would you tell me those things? How could you have not known what they'd do?

—

It's still one of my least favorite expressions. Even more so now.

Back in November my good
friend practically bribed me to
do online dating — after having
some success. I was opposed, but after
much pushing from my friend & wanting
to stop her pressuring me — I agreed
to try. ~~At At~~ At 51 years old, ~~⊗~~
and after ~~breaking~~ broken-hearted
more times than I could count,
I was fully convinced that I
would never - ever fall in love
again! Now, 6 $\frac{1}{2}$ months later,
after meeting the man of my dreams
on that very site — I am head-over-
heels in love & feel like I have
finally met my true soulmate!!
So, the reason I wanted to share
this story is to tell all that read this
to never give up on love! You are never
too old, too fat, too wrinkly or too
broken-hearted to find love again!

I was always skeptical of online dating. I thought it was for insufferable boring people. But then one day I was waiting for my friend to arrive from the airport and I signed up. On my first date I met a 21-year-old hyper-smart and extraordinarily tall Russian man. I slept with him. On my second date I met a 31-year-old Frenchman, an art historian who talked my ear off for 2 hours and murmured "mmhhh" in my ear. On my third date (which took place directly following a second-date with the Frenchman), I met a 24-year-old director who had been an escort. I yawned a lot and he took me home. I began to lose interest in the online dating scene. Then I met ~~him~~. On his profile he said he was an Ivy-league grad who had been arrested. We met in Soho. He was a poet with large eyes and the longest eyelashes. I really did fall in love at first sight. His beard was soft. He did seem a little damaged. I took him home. I did not sleep with him. In the morning I made chipotle potato lemon soup. He ate it all. Getting in the cab home, he locked it me and kissed me goodbye. I never saw him again

The kids are at sleep away camp and we are back in NYC. We were here before as a couple before our 3rd child was born. Now he is 8 and we are off to spend time together once again. It started about 22 years ago (wow). We were on kibbutz, friday night - relaxing and hanging out with new freids. You came over to sit on the seat upon which my legs were propped. You sat down - moving my legs on top of yours and then - suprisingly - you started massaging my feet. In a bit of shock I just sat motionless unsure of what to do. This was soon followed by my impending birthday and your purchase, for me, of banana chips. We only had one market on kibbutz in which we could shop, so it was a lovely gesture. On a walk you presented them to me and I - without a filter - promptly said, bananas make me nauseaus. Not the most auspicious beginnings but somehow however after many evenings of talks, listening to music, and laying silent under the stars, we had a first kiss. From there we moved forward - together in Israel, apart in the states, together in Asia and then back together back in the states. 17+ years of marriage, 3 kids, a house in the country, chickens, bees, dogs and a life we could not have predicted. Not bad if you consider starting from a foot massage and banana chips. It could be luck, it could be timing, it could just be two people discovering each other in the right place at the right time with the willingness to explore and discover what was to come together and see where it may go.

So here is to 3 more days in the big city together, thinking of our 3 kids and the next stage in our adventure together as a couple and as a family...

Today, July 5th, 2014, My husband and I got married, again. We previously married last year in May. We thought it was legal but it was void and we never followed up. Learning this we had a family friend who can legally marry us and did it today. So now I've been married twice. To the same man. And just as happy.

NYC   June 6th 2014

I died 3 years ago.
I was living my dream life, had a beautiful house, a
great job and a wonderful husband. I had
everything I ever wanted. Or so I thought.
3 years ago, my husband left me out of the blue.
I was so close to leaving this life. And my
family & friends saved me.
Today, I'm living my life the way I was
supposed to. It's not a dream, It's not
a bed of roses, but I am living.
I travel, I love, I write, I hurt and I
laugh more and better than before.
Most of all, I'm not afraid of
living. Nothing can hurt me, I survived.

Trust Karma.

Today, I'm living my life the way I was supposed to. It's not a dream, it's not a bed of roses, <u>but</u> I am <u>living</u>.

I am 3~~8~~9 ^(Almost) yrs old, unmarried and have no children. This defines me, yet it does not define me at all. Here's the thing – as a woman, choosing to not have children has been the thing that has defined so much of my life. It has allowed me to travel, to build my career, to make decisions without needing to compromise.

I never ~~consciously~~ decided not to have children, I've just allowed for the possibility that it would not happen, and never made it central to who I am. Men have come and gone, friends have married and had children, I have become an aunt thrice over. And here I sit, wondering what happens now.

Being single at 39 is completely different then @ 29 when I first moved to NYC and I felt so young and that every possibility was ahead of me. The older I get the more distilled down it all becomes. Living in a world where people are expected to couple up, and where having a child is central to being female has started to become harder. Which I had never expected.

I'm looking to twist my perspective back to the place where it does not matter so much – but in the mean time it just feels very present. I think it becomes harder to know yourself as whole when society starts to question if you are. And I am.

The thing of it is, I am now at a place where it would be pretty nice to have someone to walk with in this next phase of the journey – only it seems like he's probably looking for a 29 yr old who will give him some babies. – I guess that's not the one I'm looking for, but there does not seem to be any other kind.

In the meantime, I'll be re-exploring my whole self. Figuring out the definition of who I am in this phase and knowing that no matter which way life steers me – I'll be good.

I AM TELLING THE PERSON THAT I LOVE
HOW I FEEL ABOUT HIM TONIGHT. HE IS
UNHAPPILY MARRIED WITH CHILDREN,
SEVENTEEN YEARS APART IN AGE AND
WE DO NOT LIVE ON THE SAME CONTINENT
ANYMORE. HOWEVER WHEN YOU KNOW
THAT SOMEONE IS RIGHT FOR YOU THEN
YOU JUST KNOW. I WANT NOTHING MORE
THAN FOR HIM TO BE THE HAPPIEST
HE COULD POSSIBLY BE. IF THAT IS
WITH ME OR NOT WE SHALL SEE TONIGHT.
EITHER WAY WE WILL BE ALRIGHT.

I'm Indian. I had an arranged
marriage and I love my husband
a lot.

~~Recently, I found out my~~

We grew up in different worlds
but we have made a world together.

We are happy!

I've been trying to write a story about how I feel about being married. This is because I can't figure out if being married is what I want. But, I already am. When I'm not sure how I feel, I always write a story. But I can't figure out how to write about this. It's the one thing I haven't been able to figure out through writing.

It's not that I'm not happy. I am. I'm in love and happy. Sometimes I wish I was a simpler girl in a more simple time.

When we got married, I thought I was going to pee my pants. I' was really ~~close~~ close to it. Now I'm just trying to figure out each day - what it means to be a wife to me. What it means to be a wife under my standards.

And when I finally find the words to describe that day, then I'll know how I really feel.

Little Women

I'm sitting in a hallway, drapped in a hand-me-down blanket curled next to another girl, while an older man watches us talk. I'm rehearsing the role of the dying sister in Little Women. I forget her name, but she's sweet and feeble, and I was annoyed that I hadn't gotten the part of Jo. (even for this short exercise). The older man, an acting coach, stops me for the second ~~one~~ or third time, and tells me to breathe. People breathe.

I start my monologue again, and this time ~~of~~ the performance is different. I don't feel ~~the~~ the pleasure of saying emotions well. Rather, I'm speaking bluntly. There's no pride in my voice. My face isn't on parade.

The monologue ends and my coach nods in appreciation. "Yes, like that."

I stopped acting shortly thereafter, though I'm still not sure why. Maybe I felt like a phony, or that if I had experienced the art of acting, then I was not that kind of artist. In any case, it's my favorite memory for when I think of the word, "integrity." The same on the inside as on the outside.

I contracted herpes when I was twenty-three. When it happend, I was afraid noone would ever love me or want to be with me.

Since then, I have told all off my partners about it, and every single one of them has accepted it with kindness & understanding.

I always feld silly for making a big deal about having herpes or feeling horrible about myself because... there are far worse things that could happen to a person...

But being honest, open, and ~~to~~ thus finding understanding has made me understand that I can be loved & I can have a normal sex life.

If you have herpes (it sucks) but it's <u>ok</u>. you <u>can</u> be <u>loved</u>, and it won't be scary forever. I promise.

In 2008 I moved to New York for an internship but in reality I was running away. Running away from a miserable and claustrophobic relationship with a controlling partner. Running away from my responsibilities and obligations. From what was expected of me — to shut up, get married, have a small, quiet life & fade into banality & be invisible. I ran all the way from Manchester in England to New York.

You cannot run away from yourself. You cannot run away from your own cowardice or insecurity, your fear of conflict or yourself.

I moved back to England and I have lived in London since 2010. After 3 years of harassment and a painful court case, my ex has left me alone. After an argument we may never recover from, I have freed myself from the expectations of my culture and my parents' hopes.

I'm older, angrier, more stubborn, more suspicious, angrier hungrier, happier than I have ever been. Being liked is not the same as being happy.

Lions do not concern themselves with the opinions of sheep.

I'm older, angrier, more stubborn,
more suspicious, angrier, hungrier,
happier than I have ever been.

Being liked is not the same
as being happy.

MY TRUTH.
IM GAY.
IM HIV-POSITIVE,
IM BLACK,
IM SCARED...
IM FREE.

IMPERFECTIONS

And I write...

And I write my truth. I'm gay... I'm HIV-pos—itive. I'm Black, I'm scared.

First time in my life I am living my life. I was adopted at 18 months and my parents did not shape my identity, so, believe I am learning how to not need the validation of others. To begin building it within. It's challen—ging. Now that I'm 27, for the first time in my life I am living my truth. I'm gay... I'm HIV-pos—itive, I'm Black, I'm scared.

I don't want to fit in a box. I am a man. I'm free. I don't want to fit in a box. I know it and I know it. I know it. I don't have to... one thing that I think of everyday is how I can be more beautiful. To do strange shit. To suck a dick without guilt, to tattoo my body, mind, and soul. To love hard and have it crushed and handed to me, to write about my life in Washington Square on August 30, 2014, as the sun sets... to be bored and restless and under—whelmed, and for my spirit to be filled with passion and purpose and love and energy, and for the ends of my paragraphs to have ellipsises and commas rather that I do period. I do.

I am not passionate about it. It feels so good to be— I feel so good to believe in hu—manity. It feels so good to believe in myself. It feels so good to know I can add nobility to the world. It feels so good to take my HIV medicine, to have another chance @ another day. To have access), to have running water, oxygen to not fit in the damn box. I believe I am a man, with all my idio—syncrasies and perfect perfect imperfections, to help conquer HIV, to make good friends, to be a 1-2-3 {3-2-1}s—

I've had to begin to trust in my self out of $30K of debt. After coming out to my family and friends, feeling all of my emotions, and loving everyone around me as I am. Free. I am. Free. I am. Free.

And the depress—ion, and the loneliness, after being hospitalized for five years... After only ½ a man @ home, living in my car, after being homeless. After 2.5 years of earning $100,000 and losing some back... after spending $100,000 on an ADOUBLE FUCK AND GYNECOMASTIA SURGERY, after digging my—self out of: debt, and the anxiety, after a half @ a man, refused to go back—

just praise God... for every breath... and every struggle... and every damn mountain I've have to climb. I've seen the world... from Paris to King Tummy... Accra to Panama... and every city... where in be—tween I am @ peace with my body and my 220 pounds @ 6 feet and 17% body fat, thinning hair that my penis isn't all that big, and that my hair is thinning and my penis isn't all that big. I don't fit in a damn box.

And I moved to NYC from God knows where with dreams to fight. I've up and moved to NYC. Now, at 27, after living myself all the "wrong" ways, teaching sixth and seventh graders and realizing I'm not fit so now. At 27, after loving myself all the "wrong" ways... it's ok that I don't fit... I don't

It was a Friday night. It had been raining and thunderstorming hard on and off all day. I was hoping it wouldn't rain late that night. I was going to a show and I didn't have the proper footwear. I get out of the show, it was 3 AM, and it starts pouring. My shoes are ruined. So I say "fuck it" and took my shoes off and walk barefoot all the 14 blocks home. I feel great. Some crusty looking guys standing outside a deli see me and I tense up in apprehension. Being a New Yorker, I am expecting some negative reaction to my shoeless state. Will they heckle me? Make fun of me? No. They say:

"Are you okay?"

"Be careful out there, miss. You wouldn't want to step on glass."

"Walk home safe!"

I smile and say thank you. It was a beautiful night.

EVERYDAY ON THE STREETS OF NEW YORK I AM STOPPED AND TOLD HOW BEAUTIFUL I AM. THEY SEE WHAT THEY THINK IS A PRETTY FACE AND THAT'S ALL THEY SEE. "YOU'RE SO BEAUTIFUL!" "BELLA." "YOU'RE GORGEOUS, MAMI!" AND YET WHEN I GET CLOSE TO SOMEONE AND I TELL THEM I HAVE HERPES THEY INEVITABLY REJECT ME. NO ONE IN NEW YORK IS WILLING OR WANTS TO ACCEPT ME FOR WHO AND ALL THAT I AM. I SEE PEOPLE ON THE FRINGES OF SOCIETY BECAUSE OF THEIR PHYSICAL APPEARANCE AND I ALMOST WANT TO TRADE PLACES WITH THEM. I AM ACCEPTED BUT ONLY SUPERFICIALLY. I LOVE NEW YORK BUT I HATE THIS PART OF MY LIFE. LIVING HERE IS KILLING ME. BUT I WOULD RATHER KILL MYSELF THAN LIVE ANYWHERE ELSE!

Married my high school sweetheart.
Had a baby right out of high school.
She would change my life forever.
We had a great life, it was full of
♡ & all we needed was the 3 of us.
6 years later we would lose a baby
on Father's Day. :'(Saddest day of my
life. Two years later we would welcome
our baby boy. I didn't know my heart
could actually grow anymore w/ Love ♡
2 years later my husband wld Run-off
w/ my best friend. I didn't know my heart
could hurt so much. 💔 I also didn't know
I could be so strong, my kids couldn't see me
cry, I Refuse to be weak. I refused to break
I went back to school, graduated, even
finally got a drivers license @ 32. But I did it.
For me & my babies. Anything is possible.
Heartbreak doesn't determine you its how
you handle it that does. I will find
♡ again & all the heartache will be
a memory.

I met this girl. We'll call her "Grace."
I was dating someone else at the time.
A couple years later, I was no longer seeing
anyone and I reconnected with Grace. We
got coffee at 2:30 in a hip cafe in Boston,
where all the baristas had sleeves of tattoos.
Grace and I talked and talked. She left my
apartment at 12:30 that night. The next day,
we walked by the Mystic River at sunset (she
wore a sundress, a man in a kilt played
bagpipers as we arrived at the river.) She told me
my timing was terrible. The next week she was
leaving Boston. We spent whole days together that
week. Talking and talking. Clothes on and off. Fun
and games. But she had to leave town. We took
one picture together. I texted it to her so
she'd have it. I loved her, I think she loved
me. I miss Grace. Maybe in another life.

I once fell in love with a boy with many tattoos and a hurting heart. He heart because the men he gave his heart to were cruel, and he no longer had his mother's love to guide him. I loved him in all the ways I wanted him to love me. It was in the way I brought him tea, or smiled when I thought of the way he used to hold my hand when we fell asleep. I loved him, but he couldn't love me. Not with his tattered heart. I've moved away to NYC and I thought I no longer loved him. But here I am still writing about how I loved him; still writing about the way he couldn't love me.

if you have a "one that
          got away"
or an "ex-lover", or
anyone you miss romantically
& may not see again,
don't be sad.
        be happy, grateful
              for the memories,
                    lessons learned,
                          and the
                    spark they started
                          in your heart &
                                turn it into a
                          flame of passion
                                for other
                                      things in your
                                beautiful life.

Saturday 14 June 2014

~~So.~~ I broke up with my girlfriend while sitting in my closet today. Which is funny. 'Cause I'm queer. I called my best friend and he told me to get out of the closet - I've already done it once.
But it was so cozy. And comforting.
When I was a little girl, I used to get a flashlight and read books in my closet.
When I was in high school, my friend and I used to go in my closet and tell each other secrets.
It's always been a real comfy place to be.

Me and a ex finance (boyfriend at the time) got into a minor arguement. We lived in a 2 bedroom apartment. He decided to move out of our shared mater bedroom into the spare room.

One day after work I got home to a sound of someone truing to open a door, I quietly listen to where it was coming from. I then realized it was my ex finance who locked himself into the spare room with a lock purchased from home depot.

2 years later we broke up . . . . . he was crazy.

I want to marry my fiance. We are a gay Couple. He is my soulmate. I'm getting my masters after being sober a year and seven months. I never thought I could have anything I ever dreamed of. I have what my parents have. The best in life after being depressed, lonely and tired. Now I am not. I work in Social Services. My father died 6 years ago September 14 2008 at 1:30 pm on a Sunday. My soulmate was sent I believe by my father.

26/9 ~14

My favorite thing is coming home.
Coming home from work to my apartment, either
my boyfriend is there or I am all alone.
We have raw wooden floors that still smell
fresh and new after 4 years.
   Right now I am traveling and wont come home
for 5 months. Seeing new places, meeting new
people seeing other ways of living makes
me think of how I live my own life and
   how I want my life to be.
The very best thing is the guy sitting next
to me right now. Where ever I go with him
is home.
I guess I am one of the lucky ones...

So will you use my story? I don't know but I think not. It's a story that may be questioned or hard to believe.

Living in a small town, the new Pastor to a little Church moved in across the road. He had a wife and two children. I found myself drawn to them. They seemed to be so good together and I found myself making excuses to be outside when they were just so I could 'happen' to chat with the Pastor.

I had not gone to Church in over 20 years but one morning - after they had lived there about a year — I found myself walking down the street to church. I was very nervous - not knowing really what to expect.

I sat down in the third pew from the back. The Pastor was up front and was finishing up the announcements. Then they started to sing. Well, all my life I had always felt that I didn't quite fit in — that something was missing inside of me. I was successful, had a great husband and daughter and tried to be a 'good' person. Somehow I still felt a part of me was empty.

Well, they started singing this song and I found myself unable to sing — I was overwhelmed - & I thought to myself - this is what I had been missing. I felt a "presence" fill me - starting from my head down through to my fingers & feet - it was a warmth that filled all the hollow insides and I knew, I knew, I was home. I belonged.

Thirty years ago, my best friend came home
with a denim jacket painted with the image
of Syd Barrett. It was beutifully painted
by a friend of his from High School.

Eventually, I met her and we made two
student films together for my friend.
We hung out here at Washington Square Park
one evening drinking beer and we kissed.
Our lives took us in different directions.
Ten years ago we ran into each other at
a textile showroom that she worked at and
I was doing construction at.
    We lost contact again and met again
a year and a half ago. We now live
together, love each other and have the
greatest time. Today was the first time
since the kiss thirty years ago that we've
come to visit this park.

When traveling in
Morocco, We went to a
Berber camp near the
Algerian boarder. I got to
ride a camel at sunset over
the vast sand dunes & danced
around the fire pit with local
musicians. A 24 yr. old Berber
decided he was quite taken by me & by the
next afternoon had professed his love. He
was 21 years my junior so I just smiled &
said thank you & allowed him to "friend"
me on facebook. One year later (without any
response from me) he still sends me
love notes & sweet messages on facebook.
It warms my heart & boosts my ego, its
my selfish, ego-boosting pleasure & I
really like it! :)

Last week, I met a boy.   May 9, 2013
I walked into his coffeeshop, we spoke French + Russian +
Spanish + Sign Language.
He asked me for my number.
He called a few days later at 8pm - he "happened" to be in
my neighborhood + asked if I had seen the moon yet
that night. I hadn't.
We walked. Got midnight dumplings. Saw the moon on my
roof.
He came over for tea. A few hours later I said he
could stay. It was a few hours later that we finally
kissed.
He taught me words in Russian with kisses
Prov. (Brow) Oohxha (Ear). Nos (nose). etc.

I called out sick to work + we lay beside each other
in bed for the duration of the morning.

I cooked breakfast + he washed my dishes before he
went to work.

We acted like kids - and it felt magnificent.

I don't know exactly what happened
But I know I liked it.   We have our 5th date tonight☺

I love my mom and dad. I hate being their kid.

I love reading queer studies. I hate trying to explain why to other people.

I love helping people. I hate that I don't know why I do sometimes.

I love sunrises. I hate that sometimes I don't want to see them.

I love writing. I hate that I don't know how to make people understand.

I love summer sun and winter fires and crinkling leaves and trees turning green.

I hate trying to understand how people stop loving each other over time.

I love the world I live in, and I hate that sometimes I don't love it at all.

Hi.

I was raised in the Carribean, more specifically in Trinidad & Tobago. I don't identify myself as African-American or anything that one-demensional. I have descended from a mixture of people. Portugese, Lebonese, Afro-Carribean slaves, Spanyards, and more. Although I am clearly mixed, I am also clearly "Black" looking. I am not here to discuss my ~~cut~~ problems with race labels, but I would like to say I am in love. I am in love with the most beautiful person in the world. She's strong, smart, funny, and she has a big nose. A Big nose that I think looks beautiful on her. She's Turkish. I hope we can be together once we have our careers set after colleye. Life isn't easy because unfortunately her entire family would think less of her, judge her relentlessly, and maybe even some would disown her if they knew. It sucks to think that the person I am in love with has a chance of having her life ruined because my skin is very dark. I love her so much and I do have faith. She's strong and so am I. I can't tell where life is going to lead us, but I do hope her family enjoys me in the future and loves us both for our decision to be together.

:̈)

— She's sitting next to me right now :̈)
She's hopeful too

I am a Jew who grew up in an area with... very few Jews. From Kindergarden through 7th grade, my parents would drive me 45 minutes each way to a Jewish day school, so that I would feel comfortable with my Judaism. When high school came around though, there were no Jewish options. I was given the choice to attend any high school within our price range. It ~~much~~ ended up being a relatively cheap Catholic school 20 minutes away. Suddenly, I was the only Jew in a class of 160 (mostly) Catholic teenagers. There were some adjustments to be made. I stood silently as everyone else chanted a Hail Mary or an Our Father. My friends crossed themselves as I kept my hands by my side. Just little things like that. There was no pressure to participate, but it was sometimes noticeable that I was the only one not participating. One of the most interesting ~~place~~ experiences at Catholic school was theology class. We took theology all 4 years, and I sat silently for the first 3. The last year, I joined into class discussions. The scary part was that I was the only Jew most of these kids knew, so anything I said was taken as representative of Jewish belief. However, I learned a lot in my last year. I challenged my teacher on many teachings, such as contraception, abortion, and divorce. I learned that these religious teachings are not ~~outlets~~ just outlets of intolerance, as I had previously believed. Catholic faith is based on ~~an~~ more logic and love than ignorance and hate. Their approach to morality is just so different from that of liberal communities. Everyone has a hard time understanding each other because they are looking at the same wall, but from different sides. While I still do not understand some teachings (such as ~~a~~ restricting ~~a~~ civil gay marriage and female clergy), I have come to see and understand why Catholic teaching opposes abortion and physician assisted suicide, even if I disagree. It really is a beautiful religion, and while nothing will ever come close to Judaism in my heart, Catholicism has a special place. If anyone were to spend 4 years in a theology class with an open heart and mind, I hope that they would feel the same way.

215

Watch out, world.
The mysteries of the universe
are going to be unraveled
by two goofballs in a
2005 Honda CRV.

I watched Cosmos: A Spacetime Odyssey two nights ago with my boyfriend. It had been the first time we spent alone time together in a while, and watching Cosmos was something we'd been planning for months. See, I'm an aspiring astrophysicist and he's an aspiring computational mathematician, so we really like science.

When it was over, we talked for a long time about our lives and dreams and futures. We talked about how excited we are by science and math and education. We talked about how inspired we are by one another.

On a Tuesday night in August, at one AM, a partnership was borne from a relationship. We decided that together, we are going to make history by inspiring one another endlessly.

Watch out, world. The mysteries of the universe are going to be unraveled by two goofballs in a 2005 Honda CRV.

When I was 9 years old I kissed my best friend ████,
she was an other girl too,so I was very confused. The thing
is we started kissing in every school break to "practise"
kissing. We called the thing we were doing "kiss", but now,
15 years later I know that thing wasn't a real kiss at all !!!
We liked it , but we were (at least me!) concerned we were
lesbians, and we didn't want that.
      this story has shaken my concience so many times, sometimes
it makes me doubt about my sexuality. This is the first
time I tell this to anyone and it feels really good.
I like men now, ████ I always liked them, but this
story was over and over in my head , so sharing it
with you makes me kind of free! Thanks! ☺

Sexuality. How Fluid is it?

I had my 1st lesbian experience 1 month a go. I'm 32 yrs old.
I dated her for 3 months and during that time I had
the most wonderful connection I've ever had with anyone.
But I broke up with her as I still craved the sexual
connection of a masculine energy.

It was 2.30am. A friend of mine from a long time ago called me. Luckily, I was still awake. We are kindred spirits, troubled souls. Sleep is typically not our friend.

We hadn't spoken in a while and the call was a welcome one. I'd missed him and he me. I wanted to keep it short though, as I had to move my car the next morning. (Alternate side parking sucks) He was on his way back from the bar. We spent almost 2 hours on the phone exchanging stories and words of encouragement.

Every time we tried to meet he would blow me off. But I never gave up. One day he would think himself good enough. One day he'd be at his best.

He was finally clean and I was so proud of him. Him, sitting alone in his car, with the goal of one day turning his life around and allowing himself to dream.

As he turned on his car and listened to the sound of his engine, he told me about his home. He lived next to the highway and the cars flying by every night kept him company as he lay in bed. He dreaded the moment when the cars ceased coming. He hated it when there were no more cars. This reminded of my car. I hated moving it. But I ~~loved~~ loved my car; I'd never give it up. So I told him, "Don't forget about my car. When all the others are gone and it's quiet, don't think about 'No more cars'. Remember mine, it's always coming."

Oh, hey! (seemed like the right thing to say.)

I am a Canadian girl, but I grew up in Australia. I went to a Catholic all-girls school with a uniform that swallowed my body and really angry nuns who needed to get some. I met my best friend there when I was 12. She was my first best friend. We talked about real things like growing up and cute boys and bras. She is the most charming and beautiful girl I have ever met - her laugh consisted of really quick tiny giggles and her smile took up her whole face! Everyone loved her, but especially me :'P.. when I moved away, to come back to Canada, it was the first time I ever missed someone. We wrote each other every day and didn't even use periods in our novel-esque emails. Everything was one long sentence. In our final year of high school our emails were consumed by talk about prom night - we weren't there to shop for dresses together, so we wrote every little detail down in our emails. I remember her telling me, "You should see my dress, girl! It is a stylin' flapper number and I look damn sexy. Wish you were here - but no worries, I will dance extra steps for you tonight!" The cool thing about her was that at 16 - she had this confidence that none of us had. A confidence I didn't realise until now in my mid 20's. God she was Awesome! In our first year of university, my best friend got into an accident. She went cliff diving, landed head first, and died immediately. I found out because someone had it in their msn name. I have been frozen over losing her for years and years. It was such a desperate feeling to miss someone so much and not be able to talk to them. It still doesn't feel real. The older I get, there are weird difficulties I didn't expect. We never had first boyfriends, didn't graduate college together... I will never know what kind of woman she would have been. What her advice would have sounded like. What she would have seen and learned and loved. For some reason, that prom email always stuck in my mind. I read her emails all the time.. and have made a life long promise to my gorgeous little angel. In my life, I will dance extra steps for her every day. Every day is amazing and hilarious and a big deal. I will never stop living for the both of us, she has given me everything. Girls, love the ladies beside you the most - only they know what it is to be a woman and that is MAGIC!

WHEN I WAS 22 OR 23, I CAN'T REMEMBER, I went on A WEEKEND trip to CAPE Cod with 3 of My CLOSEST friends for A friends birthday. My friend ~~████~~ and I started drinking A Bottle of greygoose and By the time we were finished getting ready for the party ~~███████~~ She WAS on the verge of BLACKing out. Skipping the Buffet when we arrived, we went STRAIGHT up on stage where A jamaican Band WAS playing. ~~███████~~ This ended By being kicked off Stage After she kept Banging into the keyboard and its player. I proceeded to pick up Steaks off of peoples plates & EAting it with My HANds, while she kept dancing and falling All over the place. When she finally past out ~~██~~ on A CHAIR, she & I were kicked out of the party & forced to head ~~███~~ to bed, ~~████████~~

She ~~████~~ ~~███████~~ WAS hit by A CAR A couple years later in Brooklyn. I will never have As much fun with Anyone else, & I feel lost About it.

Learning for you, or learning for someone else. Which one? I spent the first 21 years of my life learning, but for someone else. For school, for teachers, for parents, for grades. Learning in a protective bubble, benefiting from the luck of birth into an affluent society. I'm just giving you very general background. I started learning ~~since~~ for myself when I was 21. Unfortunately, my best friend since I was 5, the life of our friendship group no matter the friends, overdosed from a combination of prescription pills and alcohol, plus some other drugs, depression, family shit, etc. That wakes you up. Jolts you awake. His death became the ultimate lesson for me, about life, how fleeting and precious this life is for all of us. We are all so so so unbelievably lucky to be breathing, have every little mechanism in your body work, to be born in the greatest time in human history, and to be on this crazy beautiful planet and see and experiance amazing things. It was a slow burn for me, I knew but it took time to learn and be exposed to finally understand the big picture. I broke out for a little, traveling around the world for 5 months, but came back and eventually got bogged down again. But I'm plotting my next escape, and I urge you to as well. Start somewhere, start small. One thing will build upon another. Good luck...

I am a newly minted adult who has ~~spent spent~~ spent a lot of my life being afraid.

In elementary school I was afraid that no one would like me & think my Avalon sweatshirt was too baggy.

In middle school I was afraid that I would always hate myself, and that I would never get out of the hole I felt I had fallen into.

In highschool I was afraid that I would forever be lonely & ~~that~~ that I'd never make it to college.

In college I worried about my papers due, my future career, my 8 ~~so~~ bits of scenework that I had yet to memorize &

MONEY.

And now I am graduated, green ~~but~~ but city savvy. In the months after I had graduated I ~~was~~ was afraid that I would always be stuck, that I had ~~too~~ overreached my potential. How could I, the littlest of fish ever even <u>Hope</u> to be even a wor<u>king ac</u>tor in this huge, bubbling & wonderful sea. I wouldn't even make a ~~pig~~ single dent, a bit of difference. I feared that I was stuck & ~~too it~~ this fear paralyzed me. Because I was so afraid I didn't take steps, I just stayed stuck. The scariest thing about Stuck is that it feels ~~like~~ good for a time. I was relaxing, taking a breather. But soon stuck just becomes habit, ~~impossible~~ seemingly impossible to break.

But today I broke it.

I was a highschool freshman and I went to a party. I hated parties. I disliked the music and I was always overcome with the feeling of not belonging. Of feeling like I was not supposed to be there. And then I saw her dancing.

Her name was ~~████~~, and she was the WORST dancer I'd ever seen. But then I noticed how she was having so much fun, and it didn't matter what anyone else thought.

I'm in college now, and I'm much more confident and comfortable saying and doing what I want to do.

I used to be shy. Maybe one day I'll be brave enough to tell her what she's done for me.

One of the worst things is being asked who you are, or to name something unique about yourself, and drawing a blank. Third culture kids should be able to relate. Here is my perpetual filler.

"I collect rocks."

In my dreams, I am rich, and I "gamble" rocks. Find a dealer, bargain over the raw stone, and pass it further downstream or crack it open myself. That's the dream. (Instead, my parents sent me to business school — close enough, if you ask me. I'm not exactly cut out for STEM... a friend once said that STEM fields create meaning/value, while commerce merely transfers it.)

Imagine quartz and granite catching noon-time rays like dewdrops on a spider's dreamcatcher. This is reality. I am legal today, yet still addicted to simply shiny rocks. Five year old me was perpetually cracking boulders open on pavement behind my parents back. Some opened completely ordinarily — the same dull gray (that when ~~open~~ polished surely looked awesome) as the stone's skin; some were nothing short of sell-able. Regardless. It was fun.

There aren't many rocks where I live now, but if/when one day my parents' vicarious business degree works out, I'd love to take a shot at professional rock collecting.

I just held a pigeon. I guess I haven't lived in New York long enough to be blasé about this, because this is one of the coolest things I've ever done.

Go on, judge me, strangers.

I'm holding a bird.

I actually have no idea how I got here. I am a freshman at NYU, but I'm not totally sure how it happened. Through highschool, my grades sucked and I only ever stage-manage plays. I grew up on a farm in North Carolina. I have high-functioning autism and frankly, New York is way too loud. I like this film program though. I didn't actually have a TV in my house uptil I was about 11 after my parents split. I wanted to know how it worked. I still do. I guess that's why I'm here. I miss the farm though. Especially my pig, Lola.

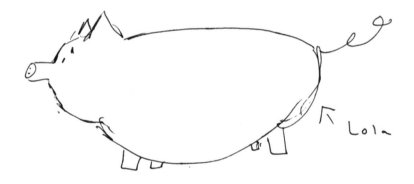

Lola

June 23 Sunday 7:23 PM Wash. Sq. Park

I'm no stranger to this park. I've been coming here, on & off, occasionally, for the past 50 some odd years. The village was the place to go when I was in college and I even lived nearby during the 1950's. The park has more people in it on a summer Sunday afternoon than it used to. But it's still a place where everything goes, everyone's okay just the way they are and as a—my friend once put it — one of the few true things he ever uttered — nobody bothers your ass.

I'm 84 now & nobody treats me like the cutie pie I once was. Small wonder, because my face is cheek to cheek wrinkles. And when I think about what I've accomplished — or failed to accomplish — in my lifetime, well, it can be pretty depressing. But I'm hoping that my being here will be enough of an uplift to carry me through at least the next week of my life. I feel a bit more optimistic about things — not so self-dissatisfied. I think it's the Village that gives you that feeling and this place in particular - This park was where a great change took place — thru the sixties the 70's even the 80's people here were & probably still are — all about individual freedom, equality — liberty & justice for all. That's about as American as you can get.

age 84. Still here.

I am in the middle of a painful breakup with New York City. It is hard to admit, especially on a beautiful day like this, where all the city's freaks and characters come out to play & you are once again reminded of what is magical about the city in the first place. I am leaving in 4 days for, possibly, ever. I spent the last year abroad & had the time of my life! I trecked through jungles, road an elephant, even found an abondoned Viet Cong prison camp. I feel like my eyes were opened. Earlier this year I was in Thailand & met the man of my dreams. He is everything I have ever wished for, unfortunately because of some difficulties with US immigration policies I cannot be with him unless I return to Thailand. I don't make enough money to be able to host him while we try to get married & get his work papers. I have to leave my family, my job opportunities, everything I know until further notice, that is until we get the money to come back as a married couple. The truth is, I am so excited to start this next chapter with the most wonderful kind person I have ever met & I can't tell him any of my fears & aprehensions about leaving. He would tell me to stay, thinking I wouldn't be happy. I know I will be, it is just somehow hard to admit that New York isn't enough for me anymore. I mean I am an artist, I should want to be here right? However, after experiencing the world as I have, how can I go back to my old life? I suppose my playground is just bigger now.... ok here we go, on to the next thing!

I just spent the past 4 hours reading through old journals I wrote, and fuck, I was an angsty kid. These are recent journals, and all the angst was for a reason, but all I'm left with, after revisiting the pain, is how laughably irrelevant all that introspection is. The feelings remain, they just matter less. Then, I lived in Boston and did nothing.

Now, I live in New York and drive an ice cream truck. It's the best job I've ever had — people are endlessly entertaining, endlessly frustrating, and just endless in number — limitless tides of strangers seeking sugar. what a way to see the world.

I'm too busy with my hands, with concrete reality, to look inwards over much — because there are generators to be fixed, and fuck, the ice cream is melting, and oh my god there's the parking cops. RUN!

Basically, I choose to focus outwards, out and beyond myself, and let ~~the~~ the world ~~do~~ do whatever analysis it will.

I'll keep the journals, but. No more re-reading.

Around 5 AM of every day, I always set myself up with a cup of coffee and a cigarette. I have a spot on my bed where I lay on my pillow with my arm dangling out of the window. Every second I spend there watching the morning come into full bloom, watching the sun peak over the project complexes in the distance serves as inspiration. A huge, brilliant visual reminder of my own tale — the shoddy improvisation of a 22-year old Hispanic artist in the South Bronx. The crisp air of the Spring serves as an analogy for the ready-to-go nature of my youth. Unhindered and renewed. Too often do my peers question their choices in life, but I find that that's the most exhilarating part of it - all of this is part of the story, and no choice, no path is the wrong one.

I suck with organizing my thoughts. But I hope one of you out there can relate.

Never regret a thing.

The world is yours.

I got new shoes. I took them to a cobbler to get them tapped, because I walk a lot. He looked at my old shoes, and asked, "Don't you want to repair them?"

I said, "No. I'd kinda given up on them."

And then he ran his finger along their sole:

which had gleamed in department store lamps
and scuffed on dance floors
they'd been shoved off in airport security
and slipped on with dressy clothes
kicked up dust on cobble streets in Prague
splashed through puddles in London
collected sand on countless beaches
run down hospital corridors, cold and shining,
disappeared under black clothes.

"Aren't they important to you?" he asked.

I keep all my dreams a secret. Sometimes I have conversation about this dream or that dream with friends or partners. But they are all lies. I make up my dreams on the spot for fear that if I divulge them to anyone... actually I don't know why I'm so scared to share the fancies of my sleep with people. Maybe it's because I hope that someday I can make them real in some way shape of form. If I let them out now they'll evaporate like a birthday wish.

My story is that all my life
I've been trying to figure out
"What the heck is the story?!"
... and I come to find out
that probably there is no story.
Sixty years of searching for
the key ... and all you have
to do is Be, and hopefully have
some good experiences along with
the woes ... and maybe in the
end it's enough just to FEEL.

Perhaps this is my story today
especially because I just came
from a funeral/memorial for
my good friend ~~███~~ who had
nothing... yet now I think
perhaps he had EVERYTHING...
Maybe we should be more patient
about How THE STORY IS WRITTEN.

HarperCollins books may be purchased for educational, business, or sales promotional use.
For information please email the Special Markets Department at SPsales@harpercollins.com.

First published in 2015 by:
Harper Design,
An Imprint of HarperCollins*Publishers*
195 Broadway
New York, NY 10007
Tel: (212) 207-7000
Fax: 855-746-6023
harperdesign@harpercollins.com
www.hc.com

Distributed throughout the world by
HarperCollins*Publishers*
195 Broadway
New York, NY 10007

Library of Congress Control Number: 2015930312

ISBN 978-0-06-238687-8

All photographs courtesy of Brandon Doman.
Design by Lynne Yeamans.

First Printing, 2015

Acknowledgments

When I started this project, I had no idea the effect it would have in shaping my life. None of this would have been possible without the following people, so to you I send my gratitude:

My family—for their love and patience while I pursued my passion, and for not getting upset that I decided to talk to strangers.

My friends—for teaching me the value of community and for listening to me talk endlessly about strangers and stories for the past five years.

My team—my agent, Sasha, and Marta, Paige, Lynne, and the rest of the team at HarperCollins for believing in this project enough to turn it into a book.

And finally, thank you to the thousands of strangers who chose to stop and share a piece of their life with me, and to you, reader, for choosing to listen.

About the Author

In addition to collecting stories from strangers, author Brandon Doman has traveled the country helping raise awareness about mental health and suicide prevention through the nonprofit organization Active Minds (activeminds.org). He currently shares stories online and in exhibits, and continues to talk to strangers. He lives in Brooklyn. You can follow his work at brandondoman.com.